# Anthology
## OF THE
# Hull Family

# *Anthology*
## OF THE
# HULL FAMILY
### HISTORY FROM 1882-2014

# FRANK E. HULL

RESPECTIVELY SUBMITTED BY FRANK E HULL II
TO INCLUDE STORIES, LORE, ANECDOTES AND MEMORIES

# ANTHOLOGY OF THE HULL FAMILY
## HISTORY FROM 1882-2014



iUniverse books may be ordered through booksellers or by contacting:

iUniverse
1663 Liberty Drive
Bloomington, IN 47403
www.iuniverse.com
1-800-Authors (1-800-288-4677)



ISBN: 978-1-4917-5505-1 (sc)
ISBN: 978-1-4917-5506-8 (e)

Printed in the United States of America.

iUniverse rev. date: 12/03/2014

DEDICATED, WITH LOVE, TO MY DAUGHTER
JENNIFER AND GRANDCHILDREN
KYLEE, DEVYN AND HUDSON

# AUTHORS NOTE

THIS IS A COMPILATION OF STORIES, OBSERVATIONS AND FACT AS OBSERVERVED. THIS IS NOT AN EASY UNDERTAKING AS SOME OF THE CHARACTERS DESCRIBED WERE SUBJECT TO BOUTS OF EMBELLISHMENT, HYPERBOLY AND OTHER FACTORS WHICH TENDED TO DISTORT SOME OF THE FACTS. SO FEEL FREE TO REDEEM WHAT YOU CAN AND LEAVE THE REST.

I HAVE DECIDED TO PRESENT THIS IN NARRATIVE FORM, BASED ON MY OBSERVATIONS AND COPIOUS LETTERS AND DIARIES GENROUSLY LEFT ME BY MY FATHER AND HIS WIFE(S). I ALSO THANK CAROL McCauley FOR NUDGING ME GRACEFULLY TO COMPLETE THIS TASK FOR THE BENEFIT OF OUR DAUGHTER AND GRANDCHILDREN AND THEIR EVENTUAL ISSUE.

I BELIEVE MYSELF TO BE THE OLDEST LIVING DIRECT RELATIVE OF THE FRANK E. HULL SR CLAN AT THIS TIME. ALSO, THERE WERE MANY CONVERSATIONS I HAD WITH CHARACTERS NOW DECEASED WHICH I CAN HOPEFULLY PASS ON FOR YOUR ENLIGHTENMENT AND ENJOYMENT.

THIS IS MEANT TO CO-INCIDE WITH THE ATTACHED 1990 "PEDIGREE CHART", WHICH WAS KINDLY PROVIDED BY THE MORMON CHURCH AND MORE DIRECTLY BY STEVEN NELSON HULL, MY HALF BROTHER (DECEASED) AND PICTURES FORWARDED TO ME IN BULK FROM MARTJE K HULL.

I CHOOSE TO PICK THINGS UP CIRCA 1880 WITH THE MARRIAGE OF CHARLES ("CLARENCE") HULL AND IDA MAE HOLSHOUSER HULL.

PRETTY INTERESTING STUFF! ENJOY!

# THE EARLY YEARS AND MY GREATGRAND PARENTS

My Grandfather, Frank E. Hull Sr. was born in Abilene Kansas in 1882 to Charles "Clarence" Hull (born 1859in Illinois) and his wife Ida Mae Holshouser Hull (also born 1859 in Illinois), my great grandparents. Charles Hull's Father, Henry Silas Hull (my great, great grandfather) was a second generation immigrant from Bristal, UK, England They had migrated West (in the late 1870's) from Illinois to homestead land and to make a go of it in the Great Plains as was popular at the time. I mention in passing that my grandfather had an older brother Irvin Hull from that same marriage (I think about 2 yrs. older) and I will address that lineage later on in the story.

The name Hull is about as English as you can get, and the Holshouser line is mostly German with a touch of Canadian or possibly Dutch from the Vandecar blood in our ancestors.

Apparently the Holshouser family had done very well financially and but from what I had heard "Clarence" Hull was more of a free spirit of limited resources. As I was told, Ida Mae became somewhat unhappy with the situation in Kansas and subsequently left "Clarence" taking the 2 boys in the late 1880's and migrated farther west to San Francisco. I have no idea what became of Clarence, as that subject was never discussed in my presence. However, according to records, he died in San Francisco in 1943, before I was born)

Ida May Holhouser Hull was well educated and very literate for a "woman" in her day (I have handwritten drafts of books that she had written-some may have been published) and was able to support herself and the boys on the west coast of

California. She was also a church going woman and made sure the 2 boys were thoroughly exposed to the Methodist religion.

Remember, San Francisco at the turn of the 19th Century was a rather wild and wooly place with the Barbary Coast pirates, opium dens and the mass immigration of immigrants, especially the ill thought of Chinese who were "cheap labor" displacing many of the whites. Also, the city was prosperous from the Gold Rush days and the vast shipping and railroad enterprises. (suggested read: Jack London's novels and autobiography)

As such, San Francisco was a city replete with numerous sub-"towns" as Knob Hill for the affluent, Fisherman's Warf (Italians), Haight- Ashbury for the Russian- Slavic immigrants, Market Street for the entrepreneurs and of course, Chinatown. It was near Chinatown, where Ida Mae and the boys settled. They were schooled from an early age in an integrated environment, mostly with Chinese immigrants. The same was the case for their spiritual education at a Chinese/American Methodist Church in the area. It was interesting to pass on that this is where both Irv and Frank learned the Chinese language! (See pictures of Frank Hull, Sr. at age around 10 playing with Chinese pals).

Things were going on swimmingly with this arrangement, for awhile.....until at some subsequent date, Ida Mae took up with the Chinese Pastor of the local Methodist Church and they eventually married and adopted a half breed Asian- American daughter named Bess. Without sounding like a bigot, the environment changed, and both Irv and Frank decided to move out rather than face ridicule from the community.

Irv Hull joined the Merchant Marines and made a career of that until his retirement. On many occasions when I was quite young, I met "uncle" Irv and his wife Evelyn (who was about 25 years his junior) as they retired to Vallejo, Ca. They had four boys by their marriage, Jack (Fresno), Mel (Sandpoint Idaho),

Don and 1 other I never met who moved back east. I mention this because there were many "Hull" 2nd cousins who are floating around there, and if anyone wishes to pursue this, be my guest! My favorite, who I kept up with until around 2005 was Mel Hull and his wife Anita. Mel was a meteorologist (weatherman) and was a great guy full of stories and could make you laugh until you're sides hurt. (Last Contact in Eureka, Calif.)

Around the same time, my grandfather, Frank Sr., somehow migrated down the California coast to the Ventura area, where he worked and stayed with one of the Ida Mae's relatives or acquaintances who owned a large farm growing mostly beans. He worked, went to school and mentioned to me that the "old man" who owned the farm had my grandfather memorize and quote Shakespeare while they were working in the fields, etc.. So my grandfather more or less completed his secondary (high school) education in Ventura and well versed in Shakespeare.

I slightly digress regarding great aunt Bess who stayed with Ida Mae and was encouraged to go into drama and acting, where she proved a excellent and talented student. She went on to be a very successful actress, performing in stage plays all up and down the western coast of the US for years. I never met her, as she passed in her early 50's, never had any offspring. I have pictures of her and she was a very beautiful woman and although somewhat estranged from my grandfather and Irv, was always well talked about.

After finishing his secondary education, my grandfather decided to go to University in Los Angeles at the University of Southern California to study Medicine, however he lacked the resources for tuition and approached his Mother Ida Mae for help. There are 2 stories here:1) according to my father Forrest, Ida Mae went to the Bank of American in San Francisco and secured a loan for Frank's books, tuition, housing, etc, which my grandfather eventually paid back. 2) Ida Mae loaned Frank money directly from the family coffers as a gift and was never repaid (as per my great uncle Mel Hull) and set up some ill-will between Irv Hull's 4 boys and my grandfather. Take your pick!

At any rate, at that time, circa early 1900's, the curriculum for a Medical Degree was a 4 year program. 2 years of liberal arts and then 2 years of Medical Training! Remember that penicillin and antibiotics were not discovered yet. Grandpa finished the program and got his degree, and soon after met up with his to be spouse, Margaret May McLauglin, who had attended school at the new UCLA campus, one of the few women to have attended at the time. They were married 1910 and my Father Forrest was born the next year on September 9, 1911. (more on that later).

My grandfather decided to pursue community service type of medicine. Around this time, Grandpa Frank moved up to Tipton, California in the San Joaquin Valley (population about 800), bought some land and some cattle and financed the whole thing with his skills as the only physician in the immediate area. Young Forrest was home schooled by his mother May, who was a strict disciplinarian. (more on this later) The First World War broke out and my grandfather served his country, but I believe in the capacity of stateside duty, because I never heard him tell me any war stories other than were gleaned from the newspapers.

Back in Tipton after the war, Forrest was being educated at a 1 room schoolhouse for grades 1-8, but often accompanied my grandfather to take the cattle to market in Los Angeles via the railroad. Grandpa often cussing about how the railroads were gouging the poor Valley farmers and ranchers. Grandfather Frank also doted on Forrest, taking him to the cinema, fancy restaurants and theatre plays while in LA on these excursions.

My Father kind of had it made....sort of! Lived on a ranch, rode a horse around everywhere, trusty Queensland Healer dog named Scout, Dad taking him to big city and entertainment (i.e. good cop). But the downside was his mother May, who was a strict disciplinarian and his teacher at school where she cut him zero slack (i.e. bad cop).

As Forrest was now ready for secondary education, Tipton had lost its luster to the small family. The family moved to Los Angeles in the 1920's. Grandpa Frank possibly did a little private practice, but soon signed on with the Railroads as a paid physician. If you can't beat 'em, join 'em, I suppose. He was gone from home for extended periods of time, but when coming home, continued taking May and Forrest out on the town to round out his education. This may be when my Father learned to appreciate the finer things in life and more on that later.....

After finishing with the Railroad medical job, toward the end of the Great Depression (suggest googling "the great depression USA 1929-1940), Grandpa Frank consigned with the recently created California Conservation Corps as a per diem physician, again away from home for extended periods. After that, he worked with the Red Cross until he retired due to advanced osteoarthritis sometime in his early 60's.

When I first met my grandfather around 1952(he was around 70 yr. old), he walked around with a cane, was a very congenial and "connected" individual, with an abundant number of friends. He looked after me (ie babysitter) and took me often to the downtown Los Angeles YMCA via trolley car, which was very cool! At the YMCA there was a plaque on the wall with my grandfather's name on it as 2nd oldest member of the club and also one for him as city handball champ 5 years running in 1930's. He apparently was quite an athlete during the Great Depression, when people did crazy stuff. It was rumored that Grandpa, with a YMCA group, had done a long distance run from La to Bakersfield (over the Grapevine Pass) and rowed a boat with my grandmother in it to Catalina Island and back.

I leave this part of this presentation with a couple fond memories of my name sake and grandfather. The first was the times we went to Chinatown in La to eat. He would grab all the menus from us, then start rattling off in Chinese to the waiters and the next thing you know food was flying out of the kitchen, all you could eat! The second and most fond was the many hours we sat and played cribbage together with him smoking his Roy-Tan Cigars, teaching me to count in my head at age 6, which helped me immensely later in life.

Frank Hull Sr. was very much a man's man. Not particularly interested in money, his fortune was in the many friends he had. He was a physician, rancher, athlete, multilingual, devoted husband who corresponded almost daily to his wife May, when gone on assignment and a dedicated father to my father, Forrest.

# FORREST E. HULL AND THE HULL FAMILY 1910-1952

Forrest Edgar Hull was born to Frank and May a little over a year after their marriage in January 1910 in Los Angeles, California. (I always used to forget his birthday-September 9, 1911!). He was an only child, I'm not sure if by choice of his parents or if there were mitigating circumstances of which I was unaware.

Soon after his birth, the family moved to a cattle ranch in Tipton, California (population about 800 at the time) where they resided until Forrest was ready to move on to "high school". From what I had heard, he had a great childhood-out on the ranch, hanging out with sorted cowhands, riding a horse for transportation with his trusty mutt "Scout" and having many friends, as other families in the area tended to have numerous children. I can imagine Forrest playing cowboys and Indians and other games with his pals. What a ride!

If I could best describe the Hull Family at this time, it was sort of "good cop-bad cop". My grandmother, May, was a strict disciplinarian (possibly from her Scottish bloodline?) while my grandfather was the one who doted on Forrest. To her dying day, I never knew anyone who could put the fear of God into Forrest like May McLaughlin Hull (or me, for that matter). When she got "cross", as she put it, the veins would stick out of her neck face and forehead and make you want to jump out the nearest window. She had high blood pressure and died in her sleep in a few years after we met. But from what I gleaned through conversations with Frank Sr., May and Forrest, it was a loving and very tight family unit. Whenever they were apart, they wrote to each other almost daily (you would not believe the bulk of correspondence I was given from these 3 people!)

One anecdote I'll mention in passing. Frank Sr. was one of the 2 individuals in Tipton to have an automobile. The other was the local undertaker. Apparently, late one rainy and blustery night, while on his way to see a patient badly in need, grandpa and the undertaker had a collision on the road to the same residence! They ended up in an argument, came to blows-so damage to autos, egos and life and limb. Never did find out if the patient made it or not, and to where.

May was no slouch when it came to her role as the local elementary school marm. I remember one assignment she gave Forrest "list the rules of English grammar and give 2 examples of each"! (as per Forrest) Well..... maybe it was an abbreviated version of the rules? But his primary education was exemplary, home schooled or 1 on 1 or whatever.


When the family migrated back to Los Angeles, Forrest had to take placement exams at Hollywood High School to figure out which grade to put him in at age 13, they decided the 11th grade! So he was graduated at about age 16 (1927). Also, might mention he was very active with his father in the Boy Scouts of America and earned the "Eagle" status. I don't know if he played sports in high school, but he was large for his age (6' and around 200 lbs) at 16.

Entering the University of Southern California next year, Forrest chose chemical engineering as a major. He was fascinated with the petroleum industry and the vast fortunes being made with the advent of the automobile and use of petroleum products in industry and commerce. This went along fine for a couple of years until April 1929.....the beginning of the Great Depression. The stock market "tanked" almost overnight and many petroleum businesses went belly up as well. This gave Forrest pause, to maybe rethink his educational decisions.

Dad took a leave of absence from University for a few years to work for Standard Oil as a truck driver who delivered gas to stations. He used to tell the story that one used a "stick" to measure the amount of fuel delivered. He learned the fine art of the "short stick" technique from his cronies, which allowed one to have enough fuel at the end of the run to fill the families autos!

When Dad returned to university a few years later he did a couple of things. One, he added a pre-med agenda to his curriculum (probably at the encouragement of Frank Hull Sr.) and he decided to play Ice Hockey for the USC Trojans as a goalie. Goalie? (makes my teeth hurt thinking about it) Forrest was always very proud of this and his "silver skates" pin that the team got for winning the division at the time (PAC-4, PAC-6??). When he completed undergraduate studies, I do not know.

Another thing that Dad talked about a lot was his fraternity days while at USC. He pledged and belonged to the Theta Xi Fraternity. Many, many colorful stories which would be rated "R" at best. Too many to mention, so use your imagination (i.e. Depression, Prohibition, Bath-tub gin, wild women, etc.)

He must have begun USC Medical School around 1933 or 1934 as I know he graduated and then finished his internship in 1939 (5 year program). In there somewhere, he met and dated a "socialite type" young woman who wrote a society page for one of the big Los Angeles Newspapers. Her name was Shirley Klogsten (sp?). Forrest liked the finer things in life and so did she, so along 1938 or so, they were married. The next year, March 20th, 1939, Shirley bore Forrest a son Stephen Nelson Hull, my half-brother.... more to follow later.

Now with WWII looming over the horizon, my Forrest faced a dilemma in 1939. Either enlist in the Military or wait to get "drafted" (for younger folk-look up US military draft on a search engine or library.). So, he decided to enlist, to be able to have some choice in the US Army and was promptly stationed at Fort MacArthur in San Pedro Calif. as an lieutenant officer in the 40th Armored Division. How wife Shirley took all this, I don't know, but she was now basically home alone with a newborn infant, Stephan. What do you think?

Quick story....when Forrest was paid monthly while in Army, he got an allowance for "forage for his mount", which confused him so he asked one of his mates. They explained that was supposedly for a horse you were supposed to have, but didn't, and got paid anyway. Typical Army....

Soon after being enlisted, and possibly being deployed to other bases for advanced training in war techniques, Forrest was approached by his commanding officer, who requested he take an exam for Joint Chief of Staff Training School along with some other officers. Dad got the one of the highest scores, so soon after he was deployed to Ft. Leonard Wood, Mo. to complete the command school. Sometime later (about a year, I think) he was returned to his unit with shiny new Captains bars on his uniform and was promoted to 2nd in Command his company within the division. No medicine and no combat so far..around 1941-42.

So here's the family dynamic around 1942.... Forrest away in Army, Shirley at home in L.A. with young Stephan, Frank Hull Sr. and May living at 939 Westchester place in the Wilshire district of L.A. Frank Sr. gone a lot with Red Cross and everyone writing everyone about every day! (Again, I refer to the unbelievable volume of mail I went through). So things were ok, I never knew how Shirley got along with my grandparents, but I suspect it was slightly strained from a few conversations I overheard. I can imagine May Hull as a monster in law!

Things get a little fuzzy here, from 1942-45. Forrest, I know was sent to Europe with the 40th Armored Division & 5th Infantry and fought there and mentioned the Battle of the Bulge, but never wanted to talk about WWII action too much, so I don't know. But I do know that he was not functioning as a medical officer, rather a command officer. He used to say that he never saw a single medical patient from when he first joined the Army until 1945-46!

Quick story...... for Atom Bomb fans. My Father was so glad that they dropped the Bomb on Japan, because before Japan surrendered, he and a small black op's unit was to be sent to Corregidor to fight Japanese....an almost suicide mission. He voted Democrat from then on! So the war was essentially over in 1945.

I do know that things were not boding well back home in L.A. Shirley, apparently had lost interest in the marriage and wrote my Dad a "Dear John" letter while he was overseas. Whether he went back to LA to address this, I don't know, but I suspect he did and probably gave power of attorney to my grandmother May. Shirley and Forrest were divorced in 1946

Forrest returned overseas late 1945-46, but to Iceland for some R & R and to ease back into medicine. I read his diary from this period and he describes his disappointment with Shirley and eventual divorce. He did retain full custody of his son Stephan, which was weird, but Stephan stayed with my grandparents until around 1947. He was also promoted to Lt. Colonel for his war efforts.

In Iceland was where my Dad met and dated his soon to be second wife, my Mother, Kathryn Regina Ballas. She was a psychiatric nurse and a Captain in the Army as well. She was the complete opposite of Shirley, coming from a small town in Pennsylvania (Robertsdale) and the youngest of 9 children. They lived on a small family farm, so it was a busy and humble lifestyle. Kathryn was brunette, reserved, beautiful and of Polish and Austrian decent. Note: I had an opportunity to visit the farm twice, and met the gazillion relatives we have back there.

They were married in early 1947 and moved back stateside, first to LA to pick up Stephan, then to Arlington, Virginia, still both in the military. While in LA, Kathryn taught Army Nursing classes while Grandpa, May and Forrest "caught up" on things and planned the future. The Army offered my Dad the opportunity to go to Medical Specialty Training of his choice free, so he chose Ophthalmology and was accepted at the University of Pennsylvania to the delight of Kathryn. (whose family mostly all lived there)

Now, anyone who has been back East, knows that the states are smaller than California and it's not unheard of to commute a few states or 2 to work or school. So, that explains living in Arlington Virginia and Forrest in school in Pennsylvania, etc. Also, it explains me being born 4/4/1948 at Walter Reed Army Hospital in Washington D.C. So, one happy family in Arlington with Dad finishing up his training in Eye Surgery, and Kathryn opting out of military to be full time Mom, Steve in about 5th grade or so and Frank Sr. and May back in LA. So far, so good.......

Well, about 1949, Dad decides to re-enlist in the Army for the Korean Conflict, so almost overnight we get orders to proceed by boat to live in Occupied Japan, namely Tokyo. Apparently, my folks told me I learned to walk on the boat (which explains my future ability to walk a straight line after a few "pops" of whatever). Also, stories on the boat of my brother teasing me unmercifully and pushing me down a flight of stairs......... (I'm gonna get that boy!)

We were housed in Tokyo in an Army section called Washington Heights in a nice officer's 2 bedroom house. Dad split his time doing eye surgery between Korea field hospitals and Tokyo General Army Hospital for 2 years. This is where he met and befriended a lifetime family friend, Dr. Masazumi Inoye, a prominent Japanese Eye Surgeon and gracious human being. The Inoye Eye Clinic still exists today in case anyone winds up there and is interested.

Japan is when I have my first memories of this earth; snow falling down, Japanese housemaids and "Nannies" and my brother teasing me unmercifully. I got the mumps and measles there, there was the "cookie lady" a few doors down and Mom had one of those new washing machines with an open tub and a wringer on the outside to semi dry the clothes, which one then put on the line to dry. My Mother always insisted on doing menial tasks such as laundry, light cleaning, etc, that's how she was raised.

One anecdote.....my brother decided one day, and convinced me my hand and arm would go through the "wringer" on the washer, since I was small and pliable.....wrong.....got stuck just above the elbow and I'm screaming bloody murder.... Mom comes out and smacks my brother....heh, heh....then gets someone to disassemble the wringer and take me to the E.R. where I was ok.

A note about my brother Steve in Japan. He was a teenager now and got into lots, I mean lots of trouble at home and on the streets. He did stuff like blow off Roman Candle fireworks in the Tokyo subway during "rush hour"and shoot out car windshields with a sling shot and ball bearings. Each time 2 things saved his butt. First, he was usually apprehended by the Japanese who did nothing but turn him over to the US Army Police (MP's). Second, since my Dad was a high ranking officer, they would just bring him home and Dad would give him a severe tongue lashing and end of issues......sort of.

Dad never, ever hit either one of us that I recall, but Kathryn was a different story, especially for me. Not bad, but definitely enough to get your attention.

So, in late 1951-early 1952, we went back stateside to wind up in San Francisco at the Presidio Army Base where we again were given Officer's housing on the Hill. (Remember San Francisco and my Grandpa 1890's-big difference).

Interesting note on the trip from Japan to San Francisco... we flew in an airplane! I remember many stops for fuel along the way, getting a smallpox shot in the Philippines which I thought would kill me (see the huge scar on my left upper arm), but the highlight was a stop in Hawaii. We stayed over a few days there and I remember only about 4 hotels on Waikiki Beach and only a one lane road along the beachfront!

A few nice things about San Francisco. First was the weather, then the fact that my brother (who teased me unmercifully) was shipped off to LA to my Grandparents to start public High School at LA High on Olympic Boulevard. Dad was the chief of Eye Surgery at the Presidio Army Hospital and I went to a kind of pre-school during the days. Short and sweet, about 1 year there and Dad decided to get out of the active army and pursue a private practice career in LA. However, he stayed in the Army Reserves/National Guard, so that he could eventually get his retirement pension which he did. (30 yrs. time in grade)

So we moved down to LA taking up residence at Grandpas house (939 Westchester place- right off Western and Olympic. Meanwhile Frank Sr. and May took an apartment about a mile away-they probably had had it with my brother who was still "Mr. Trouble".

In fact, I believe it was right about then that they took Steve to a shrink for a consult and was diagnosed with ADD or ADHD+ and decided to put him on a new type of drug called

Amphetamine, which seemed to calm the boy down. Also, our relationship changed almost overnight from antagonism and teasing to one of deep friendship and bonding, despite the 10 year age difference.

# THE LA YEARS 1953-57 &
# TRANSITION TO
# THE OUTBACK

One thing I forgot to mention about my Mother Kathryn, was that she was a devote Roman Catholic who attended Church about 3 times a week. She firmly believed in such things as "exorcisms" and the occult. I went with her always on Sundays, however my brother Steve went to Episcopal Church and Forrest was agnostic and usually stayed home. Interesting note on Frank Hull Sr.,remember raised Methodist, became very bitter about ANY organized religion. He thought churches were a rip off for the "chumps" and probably this rubbed off on Forrest.

When my mother married my father, a non-Catholic divorced man, according to the church rules she was "excommunicated". This meant she could go to church but not take communion with the congregation and a few other restrictions. This was a very sore point with her and her family, but was eventually rectified about 20 years later, when my dad Forrest got baptized Roman Catholic. Then he did service work as an educator at the local parochial High School, then wrote letters to Rome, who wrote back with fancy letters with seals and signatures, circles and arrows on how to proceed. Hence the re-marriage of my folks in the Roman Catholic Church in the 1970's where I stood in as best man for my father!

The important thing was that now Mom was legit in the eyes of the church and happier than a clam at high tide. Ah, but I digressed to finish the scene, so please let me attempt to get back to the 50's.

I'll also mention here briefly, that I never met my Mothers parents (or they would be my other Grandparents), John and Elizabeth Ballas, because they passed away before I was born. My Mother never said too much about them except they were immigrants, 1st generation from Poland. John being of Austrian decent and Elizabeth being Polish. They had a family farm near Robertsdale, Pennsylvania around the end of the 19th century. Also, there were 9 siblings, my Mother being the youngest, and 2 of her siblings died young from childhood diseases. They were raised very Roman Catholic.

I began kindergarten somewhere, Steve was finishing High School, Mom was a housewife and Dad opened an office on Wilshire Boulevard with a partner named George Laundeager M D.. George and his lovely wife Miriam, were very, very nice folks who often invited us over to their nice house located by Griffith Park and had a swimming pool! George was also an accomplished artist and made me a painting of trains which I still have today.

Start up businesses are traditionally slow, so Forrest, being the social type joined all sorts of clubs to promote business. Rotary, Exchange Club, Kiwanis, etc. and volunteered for all sorts of things. Also, he did house calls called "blind aide", I know because he took me along with him on many of these. Saw people in rest homes and the like. Funny story here-Dad volunteered to do experimental eye surgery on Australian rabbits (these are big 10 pounders). Apparently one woke up during the procedure and bit the living snot out of my Dads hands and he was bandaged up and out of work for a couple of weeks! No more wabbits.....Dr. Fudd.

In 1955, I started 1st grade at St. Gregory's Catholic Church, while my brother entered College at USC in Los Angeles. He took Psychology as a Major with the pre-med curriculum at the insistence of my Father. Forrest was doing ok with the practice, but was looking to relocate to some area where there was more opportunities. All during this time I had tons of friends from the neighborhood and school. I spent most of my time with either them or my granddad or brother doing things, as Dad was busy with work. Probably one reason why I never bonded with him.

Granddad would take me to the movies, play cribbage, YMCA, bowling, track meets and football games at the La Memorial Coliseum, etc. My brother, who had use of the car would take me to the beach or snow skiing in the mountains with his friends and other places with him.

In all fairness, though, my Dad would take me ice skating and USC football games on weekends take us all out to dinner about once a week, usually at a fancy place so I had to get "dressed up", which sucked. Took drama lessons, started piano lessons (Mrs. Pierson) played soccer and football-life was good.

Dad used to entertain a lot at our house, mostly with his Army buddies and the wives, but I remember a lot of drinking going on and I played the role of "drink getter" and got tips from some of the guys. Lots of fun. Dad also kept up with the relatives in the family and we'd take trips to visit cousins and other remote clan all over Southern California. Life was good.

In 1956 Dad started going up to Lancaster, California in the Antelope Valley where he opened a small satellite office a couple days a week. He was one of the few (and best) Eye Surgeon in the Valley and it wasn't long before it was obvious that this was the place to be. Not only was there tons of clients, but most were employed by the numerous aircraft facilities in the area and had excellent insurance.....so... We moved there in 1957, Mom, Dad and me (My brother remaining at USC).

I thought it was horrible! No friends, different school, living in a God awful climate on the outskirts of a small town, no grandpa, no brother....lonelyville. But things changed rapidly, but unfortunately. My grandmother May Hull, suddenly died of a stroke in her sleep right after Christmas of 57'. After all the services, grandpa Frank came to live with us in Lancaster. Then Dad decided to build an office on our 5 acres of property in front of our house which set back about 75 yards from the street. 1739 W. Avenue J (It's still there to my knowledge).

I attended Sacred Heart Catholic Elementary School, but they didn't know where to place me as I had been taught at a much more advanced level in LA. So, the deal was if I went to summer school, they would advance me a grade, which I did and went from 3$^{rd}$ to 5$^{th}$ grade in 1 year. Nothing freckin' else to do anyway. So, I was always a year younger than my classmates, which actually wasn't a problem until puberty anyway. Which came early anyway.

I continued with my music and in addition to taking lessons, I learned to play by ear and taught myself to play all kinds of blues tunes and Classics and Show tunes in my own style. My older brother played too, and took some Jazz lessons in LA. When he came up to visit, we would jam together and I would rapidly pick up his material-thanks Steve. He was pretty good, but I used to always kid him that he didn't have "no soul for the blues".

# LANCASTER AND THE OUTER LIMITS 1957-65

Lancaster, California is a rural city located in the High Mojave Desert locale misnamed the Antelope Valley (for no antelope have been spotted there since the Spaniards explored the region, if then). Elevation 2200 ft above sea level. In 1957 the population was around 15,000 and the streets had creative names such as 1st, 2nd & 3rd ad infinitum running East to West and A, B, C, etc. running North to South. So, if nothing else, it was hard to get lost. It's hotter than blazes in the Summer, freezing cold in the Winter (often snows) but the main thing is the wind blows every day with gusts up to 30 mph coming from the West.

Forrest bought a house on a 5 acre parcel of property on the very West end of town, so when you opened the back door you got a face full of sand. However, we persevered and as previously mentioned, built the office on the front of the property ("if you build it, they will come" type of thing). Actually, it made sense because the only hospital in town was about a quarter of a mile away.

Unknown to me was the fact that my Dad was making money hand over fist with the business. In my early years there, I spent most of the time with my Mom, who was brought up simply and brought me up simply. Buying anything new was a big deal to her and me. Meanwhile, Dad was apparently investing his money, purchasing property and hired a top notch accountant to beat the income tax man. While I thought of our family as middle class, others viewed us as more upper class which was awkward for me at times.

My brother was now in medical school at USC and I cherished the times when he came to visit. Meanwhile, my granddad's health was deteriorating rapidly. He gave up the car keys and was more or less confined to a wheelchair at the house. No more cribbage games. Between my mother and I, we managed to get him up and dressed in the morning and the reverse at night. Dad was either working, sleeping or out at night at Rotary, Elks or some other activity. Despite that, he was a great guy and had an abundance of friends and acquaintances. But for some reason, we never bonded, as he often referred to my older brother as his #1 son.

Lancaster had an ice skating rink, which was very popular especially during the Summer heat. I went there often and got pretty quick and skilled on the ice. Dad encouraged me to try the junior ice hockey program, so I did. One day, going full speed down the rink, I was tripped and went face first into the boards sticking out my left hand to prevent injury. However, I compound fractured my left wrist (bones sticking out of my skin, ugly-scared me to death) my left hand was just hanging by the skin and I thought for sure I was going to lose it. But they rushed me to the Hospital and an excellent Orthopedist named Dr. Ealy surgically repaired the damage. I remember waking up after the 8 hr. surgery, scared to look at my left hand because I thought there was a 50/50% chance it was gone, but to my delight it was still there. I was in a cast up to my shoulder for 6 weeks which was uncomfortable but still had my hand so I could still play music and sports.

It took me about 6 months to get the full use of my left hand back, and left a nasty looking scar still on my left wrist (people later kidded me that it looked like I had slit my wrist in a suicide attempt!) But what was kind of spooky about that whole incident was after performing the amazing surgery to save my hand, Dr. Ealy died 2 weeks later in a private plane crash with his new bride on their honeymoon. Thank you God!

Afterwards, I was busy with school, baseball and music. I got involved in little league and pony league where I was picked for the all-star team each year (had a hot bat). Some friends of mine and I formed a rock band called "the Bountys" and ended up playing all over Southern Calif., including Hollywood, etc., me on keyboards. We opened for and jammed with the likes of Frank Zappa and the mothers of invention, Captain Beefheart and his magic band and Booker T and the MG's.

Side note- the "electric piano" was just being invented by a Mr. Rhodes who was working in conjunction with the very popular Fender Guitar Company out of Santa Ana, California. Thus the famed Fender/Rhodes electric piano was developed. Rhodes Heard "the Bounties" play one time and offered to let me use his prototype pianos for our gigs to promote the thing and to give him feedback on performance. This I did, in enchange for getting a free piano for my efforts! Since I was not old enough to drive, some of my bandmates would take me back and forth to Santa Ana in 1962-63

Also, to my Dad's delight, I was in the Boy Scouts and achieved the rank of "Life Scout" (one step below the coveted "Eagle" like my Dad). I did this kind on purpose, I think. I only needed 2 more merit badges to be "eagle" but again without family support and the fact that my Dad always talked about how great my older brother was at the dinner table (who was never in the Boy Scouts to my knowledge) I decided to quit. Being a Boy Scout in your teens was not considered to be "cool". Besides Dad was always interested in results, not the process.

My parents traveled a lot, all over the world, but usually left me home with a "Nanny" who would cook and help with granddad. Sometimes, I would stay with friends for weeks instead, when they were gone. This, I think, and the fact that my parents rarely attended any of my sports or music activities caused me to distance myself from them later in life....more on that later.

An exception to the above revolves around Forrest's fascination with "World Fairs". These were very popular events up until the mid 1960's, when they kind of petered out. Every 4 years or so, somewhere in the World they would have an exposition displaying all the latest technology from around the Globe. My folks took me to Seattle to the Worlds Fair in 1958 (?) when they built the Space Needle and another one in 1962 in Montreal, Canada. During the latter trip we stopped over in New York City to visit my favorite aunt, Madeleine Ballas, my Mother's older sister. She took us to a few Broadway shows to include "Hello Dolly" with the original cast and Louis Armstrong at the St. James Theatre. Also, on this trip we went and visited a relative Elsie Johnson (*possibly from my Grandmother's side-I'm not sure) in Washington DC, where I had been born. I remember visiting and was fascinated by the Smithsonian Institute Museum which takes about 3 days to fully explore. Very interesting trips- thanks folks!

When I finished with Catholic elementary school it was time for high school, but the closest Catholic High School was 75 miles away in the San Fernando Valley, so a group of parents hired a bus to take about 50 of us down and back every school day. I was 13 when I began High School. I was kind of smaller than other kids in the first year but amazingly grew about 5" taller that year and socked on about 40 lbs., so in my sophomore year, I was about 6' tall and about 200 lbs. Thus started my football career. I played varsity 2 years and played against some guys who made it to the pro's. I was an offensive guard and defensive linebacker and ALL C. I. F, All-Conference 1ˢᵗ Team in my senior year (at 16)-fun stuff!

However, there is a dark moment and a story I wish to tell here, which helps explain the weird relations I had with my Dad. At my Senior year Football Achievements Awards Banquet, Dad attended.....great, finally some acknowledgement of achievement! But, he showed up rather drunk and ended up "passing out" in the lobby of the hotel. So while I was getting many awards and such, he missed it, but the worst part of the night was that my coaches found Dad passed out cold and decided to prop him up to take a bunch of pictures with him. Everyone thought it was a riot except me.........obviously I had to drive the old man home-75 lonely miles back to Lancaster, embarrassed, confused and pissed.

During my high school days, my parents took me on a trip to Mardi-gras in New Orleans with a friend, Johnny Parr, who was the jazz drummer in our band. We all had a wonderful time visiting all the blues nightclubs and did a fair amount of heavy drinking during the festival. Kind of lost track of my folks for a few days, but they were partying too, so it was all good. It was during this trip, that something very significant happened with my Father. We took a side trip to Baton Rogue, Louisiana to meet with some distant relatives named the Samuels. (I think they were related somehow through my grandmother May)

Howard Samuels was an established investment banker and he and my Father discussed investments. Howard convinced Forrest to invest in a new bank called "Bank One of Ohio" as an IPO (google this) on the New York Stock Market, which he did. I don't know how much Dad invested, but I do know that after about 10 years the stock soared and split and split and split. He ended up with 35,000 shares of the stock valued at around $25/ share. You do the math! This definitely put him on the map financially! I had no idea what was going on as Dad never confided with me regarding his finances or techniques-I had to find out later via our family accountant. My Dad always told me that he made more money in Investments and Real Estate than he did doing Eye Surgery. He was very shrewd and smart with finances all his life. But he rarely discussed money or finances with me, except to get a good accountant and lawyer on retainer. (like I'm supposed to do that working for A&W Root Beer as a burger flipper)

Back to the high school days. At this time my brother, Steve, finished Medical School, also in the Army Reserves as an Officer, and was set for his 1 year Medical Internship. With a little help from my Father's military connections, a few strings were pulled and my brother was given orders for "active duty" and sent for his internship to Tripler Army Hospital in Oahu, Hawaii for a year with his cherried out 1960 corvette. This was way cool for me and some of my friends because we could buy a round-trip ticket for $200 and stay with him for free at the hospital in Oahu. Made 2 trips over there, 1 in the Summer and one in the Winter.....nice. And without parents around! This was in 1962.

Now Dad Forrest had a thing about Lake Arrowhead, California located in the San Bernardino Mountains and we took a few trips up to there and not long after sure enough, he bought a 2 story house in the Cedar Glenn section of the Lake along with 2 pieces of commercial real estate. He shared with me later that he was very drunk when he did this, but he had that "Midas touch" when it came to investing money wisely drunk or sober. The place came with a boat dock in need of slight repair (which Steve and I did) and before you know it Dad bought a new Chris Craft 21' ski-boat. We also built, with help of a neighbor, a sauna/steam room in the basement.

We (mostly Steve and I) used the heck out of the place in summer for water skiing in the Summer and snow skiing in the Winter. My brother and I were both kind of party animals in those days and entertained many of our friends for years. Thanks Dad!

One incident that happened, though, in 1963 which I'll never forget. Dad had purchased a Mercedes Benz sports car (190SL) and loved driving the thing all over. One weekend, on a Friday night, my Father decided it would be a good idea to drive up to the mountain house in Arrowhead, a 2 hr. commute. I called a friend (Bill Pelzer) who said he wanted to go and off we went in the 2 seat Mercedes with a small jump seat in the back to accommodate me. Dad had been drinking some before we left which was not uncommon, but then he made a few stops at a few taverns on the road up the mountain to make some "phone calls". (Funny smelling phone calls if you ask me) Continuing up the mountain we were passed by some guy in a corvette who wanted to race, and Dad hammered down on the gas. At about 5000', we spun out, rolled backwards into the forest about 100yds before striking a perfectly happy Ponderosa Pine tree, which saved our lives. On the other side of the tree was a 2000' drop off. So the police, ambulance and tow truck came, but we were just slightly shaken up, but scared to death. The cops put Bill and me in the back seat of the police car while they interviewed Dad. (This was my first introduction to police car back seats which have no handles on the inside for one to get out!). Somehow, Dad talked his way out of BIG trouble, but my Mom, was livid when she found out later.

This was one of many accidents Forrest had with automobiles, usually alcohol related. In fact, I may as well bring it up now, but my Father was what we call a "functioning Alcoholic" by the time I was finishing High School. After dinner often at home, Dad would walk over to the office to do some "paperwork", and as it got later and later my Mom would send me over to get him, often passed out with a bottle and glass on his desk. Now, I bring this up only because the disease of Alcoholism is hereditary and I feel it only fair to pass this information along to my family.

This diagnosis was confirmed on my Dad's visit to Care Manor, (a 28 day treatment program for health care professionals with substance abuse issues). While there, he was examined and diagnosed by both Dr. Joseph Pursch and Dr. Michael Stone, both well respected and top of their fields in addictionology. As family members, we were advised of the condition and Dad participated in a 28 day inpatient program, then a 5 year outpatient program. Funny thing though, my Mother Kathryn rarely drank, but suffered from Depression, co-dependency and Rheumatoid Arthritis, all of which can also be hereditary.

I have to mention the "hot rod" car I built with my friends. When I turned 16 and got my driver's license, I got to use my Mom's 1961 Volkswagon beatle...a lot. I had wheels, yipee! Dad soon bought my Mother a new Mercedes so I could modify the VW any way I chose. After reading an article in a magazine about how to put a 6 cylinder 150 horsepower Cheverolet Corvair engine into a VW, the game was afoot. Several of my friends parents owned car repair shops, so we had access to all the tools, welding and workspace needed. I had a Summer job at A &W Root Beer drive in and saved up money to purchase the Corvair engine from a junkyard. Why not just asked Dad for the $$? I don't know, but I recall he thought the whole idea was stupid, so I financed it myself! We rebuilt the engine (highly modified), welded the engine mounts, put in a Porsche heavy duty clutch and Varroom.....street racing time! The "Volks-vair", one of a kind. The car would do a "wheelie" (term used in the 60's when from a stop if you revved the engine and popped the clutch, the front wheels would come off the ground!). Lots of fun and beer drinking on that project. And now I had a cool car to use for what came next.

So, let me set the Family scene at 1965 when I was ready to go off to LA to college at USC. Dad was working at the Eye Clinic and doing surgery at the local Hospital, Grandpa Frank was now in a "convalescent home" due to his progressive Osteoarthritis, Mom was a dutiful housewife always supporting my Dad no matter what. Unfortunately, Dad's drinking steadily increased and was becoming an issue again.

Brother Steve was now married to Sandra Bailey (who had lived next door to us in Lancaster) and was at UCLA School of Medicine completing his residency training in Eye Surgery and preparing to join my Dad's business in Lancaster. I had just turned 17, an honors student preparing to leave home to live on campus at USC.... nervous as hell and had no real idea what I wanted to pursue as a career in life (?music, mechanics, sports, medicine?... I had not a clue) Dad, of course, wanted me to follow in the medical family footsteps, but that was not to be....

Now a couple of things to note here. 1) after finishing Catholic Elementary and High School, I remember swearing to myself after HS graduation that I would never darken the door of a Catholic Church again for the rest of my life! This was partly due to the physical discipline by the priests who taught us (would hit us with a razor strap for mess ups) and God bless the priests who were my instructors during my secondary education, they did the best they could. I'm just say'in....2) I met and was friends with Barbara Napolean, who was to become my 3rd wife later in this story. She was a "jockette" who was a mean softball player and the "enforcer" on the girl's basketball team. All us "athlete types" would hang around together so I got to know her as an acquaintance during HS, we never dated.

# MY COLLEGE YEARS 1965-73
# 4-F'S
# FRIENDS, FRATERNITIES, FEMALES, & FRUSTRATION

Well, this part of the story is a good news, bad news type of thingy. The bad news was I almost flunked out my first semester, being put on academic probation by the Dean, with a dismal 1.5 GPA. However..... the good news that the reason for the bad news was that I was having too much fun and joined a Fraternity at USC (Pi Kappa Alpha). My Parents was very upset with me, especially my Dad, not so much for the academic probation but because he wanted me to belong to Theta Xi fraternity like himself and my Brother, not the Pi KA fraternity. Ducks in a row thing, you know. But, suffice it to say, that I rallied academically and wound up with a Double Major in Biology and Psychology and a 3.0 (B) average for my undergraduate studies. Why did I pick Psychology as a Major? I have no idea, except my Brother had-and with the pre-med curriculum I was sure, banking on my "smarts" to get me into Medical School down the road and maybe a little "pull" from my Dad.

Then a situation broke out which changed a lot of things for a lot of people. Namely, the Vietnam War in 1965. The Draft was still in effect and the only way to avoid that was to either enlist, be exempt for varied reasons, leave the USA (which some friends of mine did), be in a Professional Graduate School, such as Medical School, Dental School, Law School, etc.; or be enlisted in the National Guard or some type of Military Reserve Unit. Also those college undergraduate students with lower GPA's were especially susceptible to the Draft, so this was an excellent motivator for me the" hit the books" in more earnest rather than the ole' college Fraternity beer keg.

I had mixed feelings about the Vietnam War as did many of my new and older friends. It was more of a political war than an actual "defend' the country type of War like World War II. Here we,"the U.S. were the aggressors and instigators of the conflict rather than the other way around. Seemed that there was a hidden agenda not made public by those in power in our country. Something didn't feel right about it. My Brother kind of felt the same way but my parents and granddad were totally behind the war. "Bomb 'em into the stone age" type mentality was their credo.

So in late 1965, I talked with my Dad (who was still a high ranking officer in the California National Guard) and, despite my average college grades and pledging the wrong Fraternity at USC, see if he could do me a solid (favor) and help me get signed up for the Guard. Which he graciously did for myself and a few of my close friends.

Not long after, I was signed in at the California Army National Guard in mid 1966 and then had to wait for a few months to get my orders to go off to "basic training". These came in February 1967, during semester break, when I went from snow skiing one beautiful day in Jackson Hole, Wyoming to 2 days later being processed into "boot camp" in the swamps of Fort Polk, Louisiana. "Basic training in the Army is designed to toughen one up and familiarize one with things such as guns, tents, gas masks, etc.. But since I was in great shape from my football days, wasn't really too challenging for me and finished up in the required 8 weeks.

A quick story; the first day in our Basic Training Company, we were all lined up in a marching formation when the commanding officer announced, "I want everyone who cannot read or write to report to the officer on the left", I looked at my new friend (who was also in college) next to me and chuckled "Whaddya mean, can't read or....". "You, Hull" shouted Sergeant Rose, "y'all shut up over there, ya' hear?"". Sure enough about a dozen or so men from our company of 200, moved over to the left, signing documents (which were read to them aloud) documents with a mark or "X"! Kind of creeped me out. Welcome to the deep South in the 1960's. AND....never play poker with those types-maybe they can't read or write but they sure can count and bluff!

Fort Polk is located in Northern Louisiana, just outside a small town of Leesville (pop. 5000). As with most Army Bases, it's out in the middle of nowhere and Leesville kind of reminded me of Tijuana, Mexico, with shacks for houses on the outskirts of town, mostly for the indigent Blacks. When we got a 2 day pass, we often would travel to Shreveport or some larger town to drink and party.

On one such liberty, though, a few buddies and I stayed in Leesville and attended a "Gypsy traveling show" which was an unique experience. They set up tents and had fortune tellers, a striptease show and various performances like fire eaters, the strong man who would dare you to wrestle, etc.. It was like an "R" rated circus. We were relieved of our meager pay rapidly and returned to base early!

So, in 1966, here's the family scene. Mom and Dad living in Lancaster. Grandpa Frank Sr. was In a county rest home in Lancaster, suffering terribly, Steve (now almost out of the Army Reserves) and his wife Sandy living in Westwood, California. Steve working at his Eye Surgery Residency at UCLA. And I was in the Deep South in the acitive Army) so far so good.

It was about then that father Forrest hired some associate Eye Doctors to help him out with the heavy workload in Lancaster and began doing volunteer service work aboard the ship called the USS Hope, which would travel all over the world.

To my knowlege, my Mother never accompanied him on these trips, despite her training as a Nurse. Her advancing Rheumatoid Arthritis, Depression and caring after my Grandfather Frank Sr. kept her pretty close to home.

After Fort Polk, the Army sent me to Fort Sam Houston in San Antonio, Texas, where I did my "job" training to be 1st as a Combat Medic, then an Operating Room Technician. This lasted about 28 more weeks and then was sent home being assigned to the 143rd Evacuation Hospital Army National Guard Unit in Santa Monica, California. Coincidentally, my Father was Commanding Officer of that Unit.

One quick story for which I have to backtrack a bit, I apologize to the reader. On or about 1960, when I was 12, the 143rd evacuation hospital Unit held its annual mandatory Summer 2 week training camp in the back yard of our house in Lancaster. (Remember that we lived on a 5 acre parcel of desert of which we only used the front 2 acres for home and office) Somehow, my Father had convinced the powers that be in Sacramento, that it would be an excellent place to practice desert maneuvers. My Mother was sooooo upset about having 220 men camped out on our property that she refused to talk to Forrest for the entire 2 weeks. I, on the other hand thought it was absolutely cool as I could hang out with my Brother (who was a medical officer in the unit) and sit in on the poker games going on almost every night. Boy, I got a thorough education in the "facts of life" from the soldiers conversations going on during those evenings! Ok, back to the my College years we go.

While in Fort Sam, which was basically a large medical facility and an open Post (which meant you could go off base at any time when not working) I experienced a few interesting things. The more shocking of these was seeing first hand the casualties of the Vietnam War. Guys my age missing arms and legs or both, etc. were stationed there for recovery and rehabilitation. Also there were many soldiers back from Vietnam with either PTSD, other psychiatric issues and/or addiction issues. It seemed that the Army wanted to keep them there out of the general population, so as to not let the general public see the damage that was being inflicted on our young soldiers. Made me realize how lucky I was to be going home and back to school rather than be shipped overseas to Southeast Asia.! Thank you Dad and God!

Back home in mid/later 1967 I had basically missed a year of School, and some significant things happened to me. First, the Army had made me more mature as an individual and respectful of my family and opportunities for a good education. Second, I was pretty sure that alcohol was going to be a problem for me, since once I started drinking, I usually couldn't stop until the beer ran out or I passed out! However, the trick was not to start drinking in the first place which was very hard to do while in a College Social Fraternity -occasional wicked "hangovers" and missed classes. Remember this folks, Alcoholisms' a proven hereditary disease, I'm just say'in, you might want to be aware of this in our family line. Work hard, play hard was the Hull credo in my family.

So, I returned to my academics in the Spring semester of 1967, resolved more than ever to pull up my grades, which I did. Then spent the Summer working in Watts (51st & Avalon blvd), Los Angeles on the night shift at Royal Crown Cola (loading trucks)-though connections I made through one of my High School friends who's Dad was a "big-wig" in the Teamsters Union, which I had to join to work there. (reader-suggest google "Watt's Riots 1960's). It was a rough neighborhood and I rode a motorcycle to and from work. But I was making "big bucks" and wanted to save up to buy a new car on my own merit (1967 Pontiac Firebird 400).

What happened to my cherished and unique "Volks-vair"- a funny story, that. Before leaving for the Army, one night in LA, totally minding my own business, cruising along on the Pasadena Freeway to a Fraternity gathering (i.e. party) in La Canada, having 2 cases of beer in the back seat and a brother with me, suddenly a guy in a tricked out Chevy Camaro pulls up along side of me and flashes the "race" sign. So, not one to be outdone...I acknowledged his sign and floored it reaching 100mph rapidly. However, I miscalculated the Linda Vista turnoff and the next thing I know we're spinning out of control up over the curb and down a ravine, where the car hit butt end first (thank God!) and my pal and I wound up in the back seat on top of the beer, but were virtually unscratched. That you God! Since the car was not visible from the road, we took a vote, and the verdict was 2-0 to get the heck out of there before the police came, which we did. Climbing out of the ravine and walking to the closest house, which was about 1/2 mile, trying to look as sober and innocent as we could and, knocked on the door. A nice lady opened the door and let us use her phone to call our fraternity brothers (no cell phones in those days) and shortly after someone came and picked us up.

The next morning around 10am, stone cold sober, we returned to the scene to find the police and a tow truck pulling my car out of the ravine. I gave the police an alternate story about what had happened (i.e. front tire blew and lost control of car) which jived with the skid marks, and the officer suspiciously bought that story. Also, somehow explained away the 2 cases of beer in the back seat, but was cited for "leaving scene of accident" and "failure to report an accident" all mickey mouse violations which were later dealt with by a $50 fine. That was the good news- the bad news was that my prized car was "totaled" and I sold it for scrap to the junkyard guy, took that money and bought a used Honda 350 motorcycle and used that for transportation. I never, ever told the true story to my parents and soon left for my Army active duty anyway, so I figured I'd deal with it when I got back from the military gig.

During the early part of 1967, I met and dated a wonderful gal Named Carol Witt, who was also a student at USC and in a Sorority. I had no idea at the time that we would date for almost 10 years, fall in love, then be married later on in story. I'll get to that later......

1968 was kind of a rough year for me. I took a full load of classes and then went to Summer School to take some of the more difficult pre-med chemistry classes. It was also when 2 people who were very close to me passed away. The first was my Granddad Frank Sr. (thank God his suffering was over!) However, the second was totally unexpected- the drummer from the "Bounties" and one of my best friends, Johnny Parr, who committed suicide in Lancaster. I went "home" for both services, but was uncomfortable there now as my "life" and Brother were in Los Angeles.

Did I mention music? Well suffice it to say when I first hit college, I took along my Fender/Rhoades Electric piano and formed a small rock band in 1965. We weren't as good as my old band "the Bounties", but good enough to play on Friday afternoons at TGIF's fraternity/sorority bear parties. The usual deal was we would play and in return get all the beer we could drink and meet young ladies. Later, as we got better as a band Brian, our Bass player would book us for money jobs all over Southern California. Also, my fraternity brothers and I would frequent a beer bar in Santa Monica called the Fox Inn Ratscheller. "Foxie" who owned the place was a ragtime piano player and he would play drink along songs and urge everyone to drink along! I got to know him and he would let me sit in on the his "breaks" and play my stuff. He thought I was pretty good and offered to sell me the place, as he was getting tired of drinking all night, every night. I graciously passed on that one, or I never would have survived!

Did I mention the Pontiac firebird 400? Well, from my savings from the Royal Crown Cola job and some money I made playing music, I had saved up about 1/2 the money for the car ($2000) and I convinced my folks to put up the other 1/2 and I was the proud owner of a muscle car. This was at the beginning of 1968.

The rest of my undergraduate career at USC is more or less routine from 1968-71. I dated Carol Witt (with a few spats and hiccups), took full loads at University and would go to Summer School at Long Beach State to take the dreaded advanced Chemistry classes required for pre-med and Biology Major and partied with my Fraternity brothers. We spent the Summers usually up in Lake Arrowhead, water skiing, etc. and would spend any time off in the Winter to go snow skiing up at Lake Arrowhead or Mammoth Mountain in the Western Sierras.

I mentioned that my Mother Kathryn was interested in the occult and was a believer in the Saints and Holy Spirits, etc. I was very surprised when the movie "The Exorcist" came out, which was banned by the Catholic Church, that she insisted we go see it. Apparently, as a young girl growing up in rural Pennsylvania she had witnessed, first hand, a few such exorcisms. Apparently, my Dad, Forrest, picked up on this and decided to join a new club in Hollywood called the "Magic Castle". He was one of the original investors and members and I remember many a fun night with my folks and friends being entertained at the Club on Franklin Avenue

As I wind down the 1960's, one anecdote worth mentioning was 1 year I was made the "fire chief" of the Pi Kappa Alpha Fraternity. Traditionally, "Pikes" all over the U.S. had an old fire engine that they would use to ferry people back and forth to football games. I inherited a 1932 Seagraves fire truck which was in poor shape with a dead engine. Well, a few phone calls were made and the result was, with the help of some Alumni, we managed to transplant a big Ford truck engine into the fire truck and we were in business! One of the first places I took the truck on a shakedown run was to the home of my sweetheart Carol Witt. Her folks Freddie and Virginia weren't quite sure of me anyway, but showing up unannounced with a Fire truck kind of confirmed, I was indeed different. Which was confirmed later in the story.

Actually, I recall, with a few exceptions, that Carol's folks and I got along pretty well. I often played golf with them and was often a welcome guest for dinner on many occasions.

During 1970 and 71, I applied to Medical School at USC and a few other universities. Although having a "B" average overall during college and decent MEDCAT exam scores, I was frustrated not being accepted despite our family tradition at USC. One reason for this was that anyone and everyone was applying to professional schools because of the Vietnam War and the Draft. So, it was not uncommon for 4000 people to apply for 100 spots in Medical Schools at the time. Sorry, a "B" student was not in the running for candidacy. So my family was frustrated, I was frustrated........ I was supposed to be a Doctor of Medicine!.....but this was not to be.....other opportunities arose

# INTO THE 1970'S
# SURPRISES, MORE SURPRISES
# AND MATRIMONY

One place I used to like to "hang out" was the apartment in Westwood with my brother Steve and his wife Sandy. There was always comradery, alcohol to be drunk in excess and marijuana to be smoked in excess. I remember one night a bunch of us got totally "stoned" and went to see the movie "Woodstock". During the movie, I became so disoriented I could not find our seats after a bathroom break, so watched the rest of the movie from the back row. Another time, I baked up some marijuana brownies (which were loaded with pot) and while they were cooling, my roommates dog got into them and acted very strange for about 2 days. Anyway, I salvaged the brownies and met the gang at a "Who" and "Jefferson Airplane" Concert at the USC Campus. When the concert was over we were so stoned we couldn't move out of our seats and had to be escorted out by security. At least we had the sense to take a cab home, and come back later the next day for our vehicles!

So what about academics? I spent my last 2 semesters in undergraduate college taking Biology classes so I could achieve a "double major". While doing this in 1970-71, I took 4 units per semester doing Biological Research for one of the Biology Professors at USC (Mike.....something-I can't remember). Anyway, towards the end of 1971, having been turned down again for Medical School, Professor Mike approached myself and another student in the lab and asked if we wanted to be part of a new graduate program at UCLA, with full scholarships?

He had connections. What the heck, didn't have anything going on, or plans, so I accepted the scholarship! Wasn't going to cost anyone money (did I mention that my Dad generously paid for my undergraduate education?). What a pleasant surprise!

So, in the Fall of 1971, I found myself over in Westwood at UCLA in the newly formed program in Experimental Pathology, as one of 6 students. The first 2 years, we basically took the same curriculum as the Medical School students, then were to branch off to do a thesis on some subject related to Pathology. During these first 2 years I maintained a 3.75 GPA (A-) and each year unsuccessfully applied to Medical Schools. However, I was jinxed, never did get accepted to the extreme frustration of my Father, Brother and myself.

Now, during this time something very interesting was going on in Lancaster, California. My Brother Steve and his wife Sandy moved up there to join the Eye Surgery Practice, which Steve did. That was the plan all along, #1 son following in his Father's footsteps. What came as a surprise, was that my Brother and Sister-in Law decided after about one year in Lancaster, to join the Mormon Church! My parents and Sandy Hull's parents were both livid at this. My Father, Forrest had been taking instruction to be baptized in the Roman Catholic Church, so he could be re-married to my Mother, Kathryn, and no longer be excommunicated. Sandy's folks were staunch Lutherans and could not believe this either!

Meanwhile, Dad had sufficiently done his Catholic "homework", was baptized into that Faith and set a date for a re-marriage to my Mother. This was on or about 1972 in Woodland Hills where I was best man and maybe Steve and Sandy were there or not....can't remember

Now, not to discredit my parents, many conversations around the dinner table while I was growing up centered around jokes about certain ethnic groups, such as blacks, Jews and various others and "clannish" type religious sorts, such as Jehovah's Witnesses, Mennonites, and Mormons. It's just the way they were brought up and that's the way they brought me up. But Steve and Sandy stuck to their guns and, God love 'em, dug their heals in against the wishes of their (and my) parents.

It did change things for me, though. When I came up to visit my brother and sister-in-law, I was asked to not smoke in the house and to please refrain from alcoholic beverages or "funny" cigarettes. This was ok with me because I valued their friendship more than my habits, and spent many a night with them discussing Religion and my lack thereof. They did try to "recruit" me many times into the Mormon Faith, but I was afraid that my Mother would have a heart attack and my Father would write me out of his will. (Which he ended up doing anyway, but for different reasons....more on that later).

Now this set up a bit of a problem at the now "Hull Eye Center" at 1739 W. Avenue J, Lancaster. On one side of the office was my Dad with his veteran staff of Laurel Brewer (now deceased), receptionist and D.J. McCarol (now deceased) I, who not only knew of my Dad's alcohol problem, but often joined in with the festivities, such as the 3 martini "lunch". On the other side of the office was my Brother Steve and his totally sober Mormon staff and Sandy Hull as office manager. The big problem was this-when my Dad took time off and my Brother would see Dad's patients all was well-but when the reverse happened and my Brother took time off there were often complaints from my Brother's clients that my Dad "smelled" like alcohol often in the afternoons after lunch. So the riff between my brother and Dad escaladed.

However, my Dad always preferred results over anything, my Brother was an excellent, brilliant Eye Surgeon and the money was coming in twice over. Also, about this time, Sandy Hull, who was always a progressive and smart business woman, came up with the plan to expand the Hull Eye Center, which pleased my Father greatly. So about this time, my parents, Forrest and Kathryn, moved from the house at 1739 to a smaller condominium at 1520 W. Avenue L #1 in Lancaster, leaving room for expansion of the Eye Center on Ave J. This massive expansion took place sometime later, I believe around 1976, and included taking down the old house I grew up in on Avenue J. There was only a slight bit of resentment from me, as I never was bonded to the place anyway. Also, Forrest "gave" my Brother and Sandy a 10 acre parcel of land behind the Hull Eye center, and this kind of pissed me off because my Brother and Sandy were getting everything and I was getting nothing and stuck in my education!

The feeling was at the time that my Dad, due to his many car accidents and drinking problems could possibly die at any time, so I was somewhat concerned. However, my Dad assured me that things would be ok, and I should "trust him", which I didn't. For many reasons, which mostly happened when I was growing up and saw how he operated. His was, despite being generous at times, a great manipulator of people.

Ok, back to me and my stint at UCLA. Towards the end of my second year of my Master/Doctoral program 1973, I had to pick a topic to do research. With the help of my Faculty sponsor, I picked "liver transplant solutions" to be improved upon involving the biochemical compound "cyclic-AMP". Now one of the foremost persons on the West coast at the time in "cyclic-AMP" research was Dr. James Schaffer (now deceased), who was the head of Physiology at the USC School of Dentistry and serving as head of the Admissions Committee at USC Dental. He and I connected on many occasions and learned we had 3 things in common; namely; 1) cyclic- AMP, 2) shooting pool and drinking beer and 3) chasing women! And we became fast friends as well as colleagues.

It was to him I bared my soul and told him of my frustration at getting into Medical School over the years. He reviewed my grades and with a "nudge, nudge, wink, wink" suggested I take the DCAT national Dental Candidate Aptitude Test as quickly as possible and the apply for admission to the USC School of Dentistry, which I did. This was June of 1973. The next DCAT was in July. I was living at the time in Manhattan Beach with 2 roommates in an apartment and we partied almost nightly. One Saturday Morning in July after being out drinking until almost 3 AM, I heard this God awful pounding on my door. It was my roommate telling me I had to be downtown in an hour for my DCAT test. I freaked. I thought it was the next Saturday. So without showering or shaving, totally hung-over, I quickly dressed, jumped in my car-stopped at El Trashco for a large coffee and "Garbage Breakfast Burrito" and headed downtown LA to the USC School of Dentistry to take the exam, driving with one eye closed so there weren't 2 of everything. So much for 1st impressions. I made it just in time looking, smelling and feeling like total crap!

Somehow, I made it through that exam day, but went into a total depression for the next several weeks because I knew in my heart of hearts that I had blown the DCAT exam and things at UCLA were not boding well. They transferred me from my posh office at UCLA Medical Center to Harbor General Hospital in Torrance, California to finish my research. However, when one has lemons, make lemonade, they say. I picked up a part time job as a Phlebotomist (one who draws blood) at Harbor, while doing research. So, I always had money to party, as I was still on full academic scholarship. A lot of very, very interesting stories about that job. I'll suffice it to say, that since I was the new guy, they gave me all the lousy assignment-they started me off in the psych ward, for instance.....enough said, you can get the picture.

Then a funny thing happened, I got the mail one day and there were the results of my DCAT test. My heart sank. Very carefully I opened the results and found out I scored in the 98th percentile out of 100, for everyone who took the exam Nationwide! I was ecstatic! I immediately call Dr. Schaeffer at USC Dental and found out I was placed 6th on the alternate list for admission since I applied so late in the year.

Not long after, In the Fall of 1973, I got a phone call to get my butt down to USC Dental School, as I had been accepted, even though classes had already started. And even better, my friend, Dr. Schaeffer had arranged that I be waved from some of the classes, since I already taken them with the Medical Students at UCLA (such classes as Anatomy, Physiology, Pharmacology, etc.). This gave me more time to practice my "hand skills", which helped me become an excellent (B average) Dentist. The old saying goes- the A students make the best teachers and researchers, the B students make the best Dentists and the C students make the most money!

Needless to say, my parent, my friends, Brother and fiancé Carol Witt were excited for me and Dad graciously offered to pay my 4 years worth of tuition! I finally had a career to look forward to.

Not too much to report during 1973-77 during my Dental School day as I was too busy with school to get into any trouble partying and each day was about the same. However, Carol and I moved in together in Manhattan Beach, then we were married in August of 1975 with blessings from both families. We honeymooned in Tahiti, thanks to someone.

Carol, who was and is a gorgeous blond, had been working full time since her graduation in 1970 (?), first as a loan officer for Security Pacific Bank, and the as a sales executive with a new security company called ADP. She could afford to buy herself a new corvette, while I drove a hand me down Porsche 911 from my Brother, and we could afford to live right on the beachfront for $150/mo in a small 1 bedroom apartment with garages. Not too shabby for a po' white boy!

I will not attempt to tell Carol's story so suffice it to say our years together were dearly memorable to me.

I finished my Dental School requirements early, finished in the upper third of my class and passed the California State Board Exams on my first try. I was a full fledged Dentist! And scared to death. I didn't know what to do next? Dad said he would find room for me in Lancaster, but the vote between Carol and myself was 2-0 against for a lot of good reasons. We now saved enough money to buy a house in Agoura, California where we resided for about 3 years.

So, I went into a partnership with one of my Dental School classmates in Woodland Hills, California (about 10 miles from Agoura) I also took side jobs at other offices and did volunteer work for the Taylor clinic (for underprivileged school children).

Ok, so I was about 29-30, Carol and I are both working, it's 1977; so what comes next? Of course, Carol becomes pregnant and not long after our Daughter Jennifer is born in 2/4/78. Born down in Inglewood, as Carol insisted her own Ob-Gyn Doctor deliver the baby, which he did after 19 hrs. of labor. We were ecstatic as were our folks and friends, including my Brother and Sandy.

Oh, yeah, what was going on in Lancaster during these years? Well my Dad was up to his usual tricks and working and doing a lot of volunteer work with the USS Hope, by himself, my Mother's depression was worsening and she was more of a homebody, and Steve and Sandy found out they could not have kids of their own because they were somehow allergic to each other. Really! They had multiple tests done and it was confirmed. My brother actually lost his sense of smell and taste; which only returned if he was away from his wife for at least 2 weeks. My Father was a little 'put off" by this, as #1 son could not produce a legitimate heir to the family name. The Mormon's kind of frowned on this as Mormons traditionally have large families. So they did the next best thing,; adopted.

First there was Stevie Jr., then Stacy, then Amber, then Robin and Ryan. Problem solved. And Steve and Sandy moved into a larger house replete with a pool to accommodate this brood. And there you have it, instant cousins for Jennifer and many relatives for Kylee, Devyn and Hudson. You guys also be aware that there are a ton of relatives named "Ballas", who live all over the East Coast of the U.S. and more specifically on or near Robertsdale, Pennsylvania if you ever get back there.

So, back to Agoura. Things were going ok, but not great with the Dental Business and Carol had quit her job to become a full-fledged Mom to Jennifer. So we decided to move to a much more rural area where I could be a big fish in a small pond rather than a little fish in the large pond of San Fernando Valley, where there were a ton of good Dentists. So, I remembered my old National Guard days (I fulfilled my commitment of 6 years total and opted out in 1972) and how in the summer at camp for 2 weeks we would go on "pass". One hot spot was a little town of about 10,000 called Atascadero in Central California. So, we sold our house in Agoura (doubled our money in 3 years) and moved there in late 1979-early 1980. This is the house where Carol and Steve McCauley now reside.

Before I leave Agoura, a quick note. One of my Mother's relatives and her husband came to live in Agoura about this time and they adopted a very young girl about Jennifer's age. Al and Agnes Caffrey (now both deceased) and I can't remember the young girls name..... Al was a very interesting cat, he was a retired CIA spook (spy) for the US during both WWII and Korean Wars, and a Deacon in the Catholic Church. Agnes was my cousin, on my mother's side and her mother (and my Mother's older sister Julia) lived with them. Julia was in her mid-90's. So, there were many visits to include my parents during this time to Agoura while we lived there.

Did I mention that for a wedding present, my Father, Forrest, gave us the deed to the property to the Lake Arrowhead property? Well, he did and we ended up selling that property at a handsome profit to help buy the Atascadero property. Arrowhead was fun.....but a long drive and no one was using the place anymore because they were busy doing other things. So we took the boat to Atascadero and I used the proceeds from Arrowhead to build out a Dental Office in a Center on El Camino near San Anselmo and the rest of the money in savings.

Does this pattern sound familiar.... my Dad leaving LA for Lancaster and Me leaving Agoura for Atascadero.......I'm just say'in.

# 1978-80
# FORREST THE POLITICAN AND BROTHER STEVE'S POWER PLAY

I apologize to the readers for length, but I would not be doing my due diligence if I glossed over a few family issues. On or about 78'-79', 3 significant things occurred, 1 of which really upset the apple cart for our family.

The first being my Father deciding to run for City Council in the newly formed "city" of Lancaster. (before it was only a "town"). He recruited my brother and I to help him campaign, which was time consuming and Steve and I were both really busy and didn't really have time for this. But, family is family and so.... you help when asked. Forrest ended up winning the election and was now one of the original Councilmen and helped form the new City Charters and bye-laws.

This was great, we were all proud of Forrest's accomplishment. However, a problem arose, because they Issued Councilman Hull a shiny Gold Badge to wear and a snub nosed .38 revolver, which made everyone a little nervous, because we felt that someone who was now drinking about a fifth of booze a day, could possibly be trusted with a loaded firearm in the house. We we're not gun people but we nervously we went along with Dad's wishes to keep a loaded gun in the house because of the "Golden Rule- which was-" he who has the Gold, makes the rules!"

The second thing was that Dad finally retired from the Army as a full Colonel, now eligible for his retirement pay which was about $3200/ month. Now, Dad's net worth here was about

5 million dollars then anyway, and this helped him focus less on Eye Surgery, but traveled all over the world, doing Eye service work several times a year, leaving Mom at home and Steve in charge of the Lancaster office. Also, Forrest was a bit of an enigma to me, because I never really understood how a guy with his skill set, could drink almost s fifth of whiskey a day could function...at all, day after day. Never did figure that out! Baffling!

Which leads into #3 situation. Brother Steve and my Mom had finally had it with Dad's drinking and turned him over to the State Medical Board as "unfit to practice Medicine". Man, did the cow dung hit the fan on this one! Under threat of losing his Medical License, my Dad was ordered to 28 day rehab and have a 5 year follow up of aftercare to keep his license. Forrest went to the rehab, but was sooo mad that it really didn't take. Now, when Forrest E. Hull got mad, he didn't show it, but concocted a plan to get even, which he did, indirectly.

Since my Mother and Brother didn't drink, but I did (to excess), Dad turns me over to the State Dental Board for the same reason as above! What's up with that! Next thing you know, I'm in a 28 day rehab with a 5 year follow up! That freak'in weasal! He also had me see a Psychiatrist, who was convinced I had a brain tumor, which later proved false.

However, I'm sad to report that the supposed "cure" didn't take for either of us, though we never got caught by the powers overlooking our cases and nobody lost their licenses. Thank you God!

# INTO THE 1980'S
# REHABS, RECOVERY
# AND RELOCATION.....

OK, I admit I had a serious drinking problem, living in Atascadero. I can sum up my pathological actions in a few sentences. 7 DUI's, 10 more rehabs (which didn't work) and a very upset Carol Witt Hull. When I was sober, I was right on and very productive as a Dentist. However, during any given year, if you looked at my appointment book, I only worked about 8 months out of the year. This was due to either having to be in rehab for a month or 2 and/or jail for a DUI, or just drunk or hung-over too bad to go into the office. (I was later diagnosed alcoholic, bipolar and ADD, and have been on medication in recovery since I was 40 years old)

Although, when I was "on", the money rolled in and I eventually bought an acre of prime commercial property in Atascadero in partnership with my Mom and Dad. The idea was to eventually develop or sell the land for a profit. Carol and I worked with an Architect and Engineers and drew up the plans for developing that property, where my new office would become part of a 10 unit complex. Dad would finance the construction and we would split the proceeds, or so we thought. Remember, my Dad was a very shrewd and tough negotiator. But, then I would be financially set for life-just show up for work. This complex is still at the corner of El Camino and San Anselmo and called the "San Anselmo Center", although we don't own it anymore, check it out kids

I also landed a few lucrative contracts with big groups of Dental clients. One of these was the Retail Clerks Union for all of San Luis Obispo County, about 2000 members. My little office was getting too small. Besides, what could possibly go wrong??

When Jennifer turned 6, she started kindergarten at public school in Atascadero and I fondly remember driving her over there in the mornings in my shinny new Mercedes automobile. Carol had decided to go back to work, but wasn't sure what would work in a small town. So, we thought about it and listened to people complain about Ambulances and Fire trucks and Police often having trouble locating a call for help due to inadequate signage on streets. That was it! We started a reflective signage business out of our home garage and with a little advertising, the business took off. Carol soon rented a small commercial business office, and that was the birth of the Sign Outlet Business, which she worked until retirement.

In all fairness, we did go on family vacations to Hawaii and to a World's fair in Canada, but I believe Jennifer was too young to remember these trips. However, after a few years of my erratic behavior, one tends to wear people out, especially those close to you as Carol, Jennifer, my office staff, my parents and patients. Carol gave me too many second chances to count... but I COULD NOT STOP DRINKING!!

She finally and rightfully, divorced me in 1987 and I can't blame her. My parents un-inherited me, I lost my Dental contracts, the commercial property (to my parents) and eventually the house on San Gabriel Road and my Dental Office. Lost almost everything except my life and a boat and a few Dental Supplies.

Now, Jennifer was very upset at the divorce, she was about 8-9 when it all happened. As a result, she kind of blocked out (or so she says) a lot of her Childhood. She of course, stayed to live with her Mother in Atascadero, while I moved down to Santa Barbara to seek treatment for my addiction to Alcohol. I did not work as a Dentist for 2-3 years, I didn't trust myself and was ashamed at what I had happened.

So here's a snapshot of the Hull family in 1988. My Brother and Dad are working together in Lancaster, my Brother expanded the small original office into a giant Eye Center, aptly called the Hull Eye Center. It was complete with 2 operating rooms and a staff of around 25 people. My sister-in-law, Sandy, was the office manager and Dad was semi-retired. Did my Dad stop drinking? No! What a hypocrite!

My Brother was a pioneer in eye surgery, one of the few doctors performing the new Lasic type surgery. (which was called "Radial Keratotomy" at the time). He consulted with another Ophthalmologist from Santa Maria named Dennis Sheppard, MD who was also a pioneer in the same surgery. He and his wife, Francia, became fast friends with my brother and Sandy and more on this later. Meanwhile their adopted kids are growing up and doing fairly well, except Stevie Jr., more on that later also.

My Mother, Kathryn (or Kitty, as she was nicknamed) was now a bedridden invalid requiring round the clock nursing care at home at the condo in Lancaster. She suffered greatly for years and my heart goes out to her even today, she was a fine woman and the closest to me of the my parents.

Meanwhile, I am financially broke, turning 40, single, living in a half way house in Santa Barbara. I also had my driver's license restricted for 5 years and was facing a 1 year in jail and a substantial court fine for my last DUI. I was driving an $800 used car when I could. Swell, eh? But something remarkable happened to me then. Not practicing Dentistry now and attending Alcoholic Anonymous meetings in "huge" Santa Barbara, I stopped drinking!!!!! With the exception of a few hiccups, for all intents and purposes, I was done.....suffering over.

I took a minimum wage job in Goleta for 2-3 years with Alcon Surgical as a technician and salesman. $6.00/hr whoopee! I was re-creating myself, estranged from old family and friends and thanks to my new found friends in recovery. I kept in contact with Carol and Jennifer but avoided my parents as much as possible. My Dad would call me once a week and ask "Are you working as a Dentist yet?" To which I would answer no, then he would proceed to remind me that I was cut out of his will. Eh, nice guy!

I had just about enough money to live on and that was it. Maybe a $20,000 retirement fund, but I owed the bank $40,000 on credit cards. So, I was upside down, financially. No money for dating or trips etc., just Recovery from the disease of Alcoholism.. Meanwhile Carol found a friend Steve McCauley, nice guy, who she was casually dating and she would bring Jennifer down for "visits" about once a month.

As a salesman at Alcon I got some perks to include insurance, etc and an opportunity to travel to conventions to work on the floor doing sales. Ironically, I was selling mostly Eye Surgery equipment and met my brother Steve and Dennis Sheppard at a few conventions. I got to travel for free (paid for by Alcon) to places like Las Vegas, New Orleans and Singapore for these conventions-all expenses paid. I did well in sales and they wanted to promote me, but that meant moving to Fort Worth, Texas, which I didn't want to do. So after 3 years, I resigned and eased back into Dentistry in Santa Barbara.

# 1989-93
# LOSS OF FAMILY
# AND FRIENDS

Now just because my Brother, Steve, and I were separated geographically and religiously, didn't mean we weren't still close. In fact, he was my best friend and mentor for years and years-he never gave up on me when the rest of the family did. So, when he suddenly died of a heart attack in 1989,at age 51, I was shocked and still am. When I got the phone call, I thought it was a bad joke, while other relatives got confused and thought it was me that died, since I had so many problems. Steve didn't smoke or drink and ate well and was a slim 160lbs opposed to my 220 lbs. My parents, staff at the Eye Center, Sandy and kids, etc. were all numb with shock and sadness, as was I.

I remember it was right before Thanksgiving when he passed in the prime of his Career. My Dad was especially shaken, #1 son gone now and he retreated to the bottle again, I did not. I made a beeline trip to Lancaster and stayed for a week, mostly with Sandy and the kids, asking what I should do to help? Sandy asked me to look after my Father, try to keep him sober and entertain the kids as much as possible. Carol and Jennifer came over as well.

This was the longest week of my life and the worst Thanksgiving ever. He passed on the Sunday before Thanksgiving, but an autopsy had to be performed and then Thursday a Holiday, so the Funeral was set for Friday at the local LDS Church, where Steve had served both as "bishop" and "stake president" over the years. I tried to keep Dad sober, but failed. But did manage to help Sandy with the Kids, etc. There were over 1000 people at the Funeral (I should be so lucky) and I was a pall bearer to my Brothers coffin. He was laid to rest in Lancaster and I often visit his gravesite still to this day. My Father could not even speak at the funeral, he was so shaken.

So, I'll shift gears real quick before delving back into the more depressing history. Back in Santa Barbara, I picked up 3 Dental jobs and went back to work, living in a small apartment on Micheltorena St. near St. Francis hospital on the Riviera. I had a sober roommate (Dale Brothers) who also worked full time as a CNA male nurse. We were close friends as well. So one day out of the blue, minding my own business- there's a knock on my door? I open it and who stands there but my Daughter, Jennifer, with 2 suitcases in her hands. Right behind her are Carol and Steve McC, with a rollaway bed. They say, "we can't take it anymore, she's living with you for awhile"! My mouth was agape, this whole scene lasted about 1 minute and Steve and Carol left, leaving Jennifer in my care.

OK.....now what? How to explain to my roommate and girlfriend Annie Methot (Sober 15 yrs.)? What about school? A thousand questions went through my head in 30 seconds! Meanwhile, Jennifer plops on the couch and with a snotty attitude says "got anything to eat around here"? Let me paint a picture here-my daughter who is now 12 is dressed in a gang banger outfit, replete with men undershorts hanging out and Levi's which are about 6 sizes too big so they hang off her waist, and a flannel shirt. Get the picture? Defiance in Aces. This was 1990.

So, I did what I could, thankfully she "took" to both my Roommate Dale and my girlfriend Ann, and I enrolled her with some difficulty, at Santa Barbara Junior High School. Little did I know this was to be the longest 2 years of my life, but the most rewarding. It wasn't long before I started getting calls from the Junior High School about my daughter's misconduct once a week. This was to continue as well as $400 phone bills for awhile, due to Jennifer calling her friends up in Atascadero, Paso Robles area- long distance calls!

Lest I forget Lancaster-after my brother passed, my Dad and Sister- in- Law got into it, big time. Forrest wanted to donate the Hull Eye Center to UCLA or USC Schools of Medicine for a remote teaching facility. However, Sandy, who owned majority interest in the Hull Eye Center, had a buyer lined up to purchase the business. Sandy won out, atta girl, and then immediately moved to Provo, Utah with all the kids, leaving my Dad and Mom pretty much by themselves. Meanwhile, #2 son (me) was also pretty much estranged from my parents, being dis-inherited and harassed over the years and all will do that to you!

Meanwhile back in SB, I have my hands full with my daughter and work, trying to keep her in school and somehow graduate from Junior High. She eventually is moved forward, Ok-done. Now to High School-but where? There's the public High, but I'm afraid she'll do the same thing, so I check out private schools. I have a few bucks from my Dental working now and can afford this luxury. After a few hiccups, we get Jenn enrolled at Immaculate Heart High, in a small class of about 15 kids. And it seems to do the trick! Almost overnight, my Daughter's personality and grades changed for the better and our relations improve.

One anecdote: On Easter of the second year with me, I took out Jenn to buy a new Easter Dress, which looked great and bought myself a new suit to match. We made reservations at the Biltmore for Easter Brunch and just the 2 of us got up Easter morning went to Church (I think) then went to the Biltmore to eat. It was a beautiful Santa Barbara day and we were a dashing couple! We spent it seemed like all day at the Hotel picking and snacking and talking and just enjoying each other's company.

One of the most intimate encounters I've ever had with another human. Serious bonding happened that day for me.

Jennifer's grades improved dramatically from a C- in Junior High to A's and B's in the private High School. Also, we "hung out" together more going to concerts together, stage plays and movies. I had switched girl friends due to my increased interest in the Christian religion and Ann's lack thereof, and met and dated a new friend named Nancy (not real name), a Christian woman who was just getting out of a 1 yr. rehab for Cocaine addiction and was a gorgeous brunette, who bonded with my Daughter.

I also might mention that I attended almost daily AA meetings and Jennifer got interested in the Alateen program for teenagers. In fact Jennifer was the Keynote speaker at the annual AA convention, giving a 1 hr. talk in front of about 100 people, mostly blasting me. But I didn't care, I was proud of her for her efforts and talents. I was also a keynote speaker at the convention but in another group of about 500.

So into late 1992, I had another of those funny knocks on my door, minding my own business. This time it was a gentleman in a suit and asked if "Frank Hull the Dentist" lived there. Thinking it was a process server with some warrant over old DUI's, I replied, "who wants to know". The man explained he was from an insurance company and had been trying to find me for 2 yrs. It was regarding an old disability policy I had taken out in 1977 and kept current until 1987. I invited him in and we had coffee. He explained that the company he represented wanted to buy out my policy, which would be paying me $4000/ mo. until I was 65 unless I took the money now. We negotiated a bit and came to $250,000 dollar offer! He cut me a check that day and within a week I purchased a house in Mission Canyon area of Santa Barbara (2944 La Combadura Rd.) and we all moved there. Myself, Jennifer, Dale and Nancy and another sober friend Warren.

Soon Nancy and I were engaged to be married, but it was not meant to be.....my Mother's health was really failing so Jennifer and I went over to Lancaster to visit her on a Sunday, October 12, 1992. Mom was in bad shape, weighing only about 80 lbs. and could barely talk. Jennifer and I held her hand for about 10 minutes while I silently prayed for God to end this suffering. We visited with Dad a bit, told him about the new address and phone #, etc. then left so we could be back for Monday work and school.

When we got back home, Nancy was gone with my other car, and left a note saying she was leaving me for her old boyfriend! I was crushed and so was Jennifer. The next morning I got the phone call from my Dad telling me my Mother had passed away in the night and to get over to Lancaster for the services. Now, I was double reeling; my fiancé gone with my car, my Mother suddenly dead and having to deal with cancelling the week for both myself and Jennifer so we could get back over to Lancaster. I flipped out and started drinking again, not much, but enough to get my daughter's disappointed attention.

At my Mother's Services, which were lightly attended mostly because mother Kathryn's relatives were mostly on the East Coast and many other friends had died, so it was mostly immediate family. As her wishes, she was buried at a military cemetery in Riverside, California. But Jennifer's mother Carol and Steve McCauley were there and took one look at me and knew what was up with my drinking, again. So after the services, Jennifer went back to stay in Atascadero with her Mother Carol. I hung around with my Dad for a day or 2, both of us drinking and then I sobered up and made it back to Santa Barbara for the weekend and to figure out the mess with Nancy, etc; hating myself for losing custody of my daughter again. Dale said he hadn't heard a word from her or seen her all week! So, I checked my phone messages and the police had towed my car, so I had to bail out my car. I never saw or heard from Nancy again....wow!

After all was sorted out, I threw myself into my Dental work and decided to open my own private office called Mission Dental in Santa Barbara. I financed this by taking out a mortgage on my house and found a suitable facility at 525 E. Micheltorena on the top floor overlooking the city and ocean. I secured several lucrative insurance contracts and started making money hand over fist right from the beginning. This was in 1993-2000.

The Dentist next door was not very happy that I open a competitive business, but after a while, we became friends and he had a cute Dental assistant named Jessica (not real name) who was a nice looking blond. She was from Wales, England and working on a permanent "green card" as a resident, but had a British Passport. I had my eye on her and we eventually dated and were married in 1995. She and her 2 teenage sons moved into my house in Mission Canyon.

In 1996, I was approached by a realtor friend who told me to drop what I was doing and come look at this house on the top of the Riviera overlooking the Pacific Ocean. The banks had foreclosed on the large property and it was up for a 'sealed auction bid" (google this if you wish). My Bid turned out to be the highest ($300,000) and after so negotiations with the bank, I talked them down to $275,000 because of outstanding building permits, the bank took it. Now I owned 2 houses in Santa Barbara.

So Jessica and I and the 2 boys, Thomas (not real name) (17) and Stan (not real name) (14) moved into the new house at 1141 Arbolado, SB and I rented out my other house. So my net worth now was about $2 million, with the business, invested savings, stock market portfolio and Real Estate Holdings.

In 1998, I first threw my back out and had to have the first of several back surgeries. I continued to work, but took on 2 associate Dentists to help with the work load. I had to cut down to 3-4 days a week. Then in 2000, Jessica and I were not getting along (she was drinking and doing drugs behind my back) and so I divorced her in 2000. Also in 2000 I had my second back surgery and decided to sell Mission Dental for health reasons. I was paid $500,000 for the business and I sold the house up on the Hill for $ 1.3 Million, less the mortgage, which netted me around another $750,000 when the dust cleared with the divorce and taxes.

Since my old house was "leased out" for a year, I could not move back in right away, so I moved in with an old fishing buddy in Solvang, California for about 6 month, put all the furniture in storage and commuted to work 4 days a week, as an associate Dentist in Santa Barbara again.

After Mom passed away, Dad, who was now in his early 80's decided to find some additional female companionship. He first dated a widow he met at the Hollywood High School 75th reunion, then a few local widows, then developed a relationship with Martje Van Wackem, (now deceased, I believe) who was 10 years younger than Forrest. She was Canadian/Dutch having been previously married to a "Royal Dutch Petroleum" big wig and lived in Vancover Canada, British Columbia. They had apparently met several years before during one of Forrest's volunteer service projects, became friends and she was eventually widowed. It was a long distance on again off again type of relation, but gave Dad something to do in the late 1990's.

Now, apparently, Martje also owned a piece of vacant land in a small town of Kaslo, British Columbia-right on a Lake Front. That was all that Forrest needed! With money to burn, he talked Martje into building a large custom house on the property for family and friends to use. This he did, and Jennifer and I visited him there every year on his birthday in September, thinking each trip may be the last time we saw him. Hah, Forrest lived to be 93! (remember, born in 1911) You do the math.....so we took many road trips to Kaslo annually. Beautiful place, with gorgeous views, but lousy fishing and not much to do-very remote. I mention this because to the best of my knowledge Jennifer Hull and myself were the only other Hull's to ever see the place! The Van Wachem clan used the place most of the time as they were closer geographically.

# 2000-2010
# DAD'S PASSING AND MORE BACK PROBLEMS, AND....

Did I mentioned that my Dad, Forrest got married for a 3rd time? Well he did- to the Dutch lady named Martje Van Wakem. They were married in 2002 on Feb 4th (Jennifer's birthday)!Martje and I got along pretty well, however, I really didn't get to know her as she and my Dad traveled a lot.. But she did care for my Dad, so I'm very grateful to her for that.

Back in early 2001-living in Solvang, and before my Dad got re-married, I spent a lot of time on the computer and visited a site called "Classmates.com". I touched base with some of my college and high school friends. One of my High School classmates lived in nearby Carpinteria, so we decided to meet for lunch at a place and talk about old times. Her name was Barbara Gardner? I didn't really remember her from High School then she mentioned her maiden name was Napolian, which then I remembered.

Barbara and I became "friends" and I would sometimes stay at her place overnight in Carpinteria, rather than commute back to Solvang, during the work week. She was, and is, a good looking blond, who can cook and make me laugh. Eventually, I moved back into my house in Santa Barbara when the "lease" was up and I and Barbara were now living only about 20 miles apart from each other. But, I was still reeling from my second divorce and was not looking for any permanent relations with the opposite sex.

Meantime, in 2001, I was getting concerned about my Dad. I would get numerous phone calls from friends and employees of my Father in Lancaster saying things like, "you better get over here right away, your Father is in the hospital with……", things such as mild heart attack, slip and fall accident or out of control with his drinking. Now, I was working 5 days a week and taking time off to run over to Lancaster every month or so and was getting my employers a little upset, but I did what I had to do for family and made those several trips to check up on Forrest. The final such trip was a biggie, as Dad was in Ft. Lauderdale, Florida on a cruise with Martje and friends and had a Major heart attack. I was called… dropped what I was doing and flew to Florida and rented a room next to the Hospital where Dad was in the Critical Care Unit, not expected to make it. He was a mess when I first saw him and after talking to the excellent Cardiologist taking care of him, was very concerned. I was there for about 10 days.

However, Dad rallied and after a few days was conscious and talking and apparently well on his way to recovery and leaving the Hospital. One cute story here- after Dad was much better but still in the Hospital, I visited and asked him if I could get him anything? He joked with me that his blood alcohol level was getting dangerously low, and he also wanted some "mizzo soup" (a Japanese soup loaded with salt) and not good for a cardiac patient. But as a dutiful son, I got Dad a small bottle of Vodka, some orange juice and the mizzo soup later in the day and snuck it into his room. The next day, I showed up to see my Dad out of bed, dressed in his suit sitting up doing "paperwork" wanting to know when he could get out of this place and back home to Lancaster? An overnight miracle! So the message is …always listen to what your body tells you to eat or drink despite what is going on with your health.

Now getting Dad and Martje out of Florida and on a plane to fly back to California was no easy task. Dad needed oxygen on the flight, Martje had messed up her knees apparently so both of them were in wheelchairs. 9/11 had just happened (google 9/11 and the twin towers in New York City) and airport security was unbelievably "tight". We got 1st class seats for them, but had to arrive at the airport 4 hours before the flight for security to check bags, etc. Even when we entered the parking structure at the airport, we were stopped by police, who went all over the car and had a "bomb sniffing dog" check us out! Suffice it to say, they barely made their flight and I called Los Angeles to have a friend arrange for them to get picked up and taken to Lancaster. Whew! What an ordeal...and expensive!

I returned home to a few upset employers, but talked my way back into their good graces and after a few weeks, all was forgotten and well with my work.

Again, I digress to mention that my (our) daughter Jennifer had gone to Catholic High School in San Luis Obispo, except for her senior year, when she decided to finish High School in Utah, close to her cousins for a year, especially Amber Hull. After that, she was working part time and Carol and I were paying for her to attend College Classes which she did part-time. So she didn't really live with me since my Mother had passed away some time back, she was in or around Atascadero, doing OK. I also took Jennifer with me on numerous fun vacations to La Paz, Mexico, which I will let Jennifer tell you about!

Meanwhile, I was now experiencing some health issues of my own, kind of 2 fold. First, my back was really bothering me, and the Doctors decided that I needed another surgery, which I did and was out of work 6 weeks in recovery and on medication. Also, I had been getting very Depressed about life in general for numerous reasons, so I went to a hot shot Psychiatrist in Santa Barbara who ran a bunch of tests and concluded I was "Bipolar" and put me on various other medications!

Co-incidentally the same day I had back surgery in Santa Barbara my new friend Barbara was also having surgery, having a cardiac stent placed in her heart. So she was recovering from that while I was recovering from back surgery. Also, did I mention that she also suffered from clinical depression, so we now had more in common?

Fast forward to 2004. In February, Barbara and I decided to get married while on a trip to La Paz, Mexico and were married there while on the trip. This was my 3rd marriage (gee.., what a co-incidence, both my Father and I were married 3 times!) So she moved in with me at my house in Mission Canyon, Santa Barbara. Then in mid- October 2004, my Father was in Canada with Martje and I got phone calls from him saying how much he appreciated all I had done for him and that he really loved me. I knew something was up....very unusual coming from Dad... and sure enough, he was saying his "goodbyes" to me and sure enough a week later he passed away at the age of 93, at lunch with friends in Canada. Just fell out of his chair and had the big heart attack. Sad.......but inevitable, we all have to go through death. The old "bear" had finally met his match.

Now this presented several problems, as since Dad died out of the country, I had to physically go up there with Barbara and get all the affairs to release the body in order with the help of Martje, who was totally out of it with grief and non-functional. Flew to Alberta, Canada, got a hotel room, and worked with Martje's daughter Yolanda, who was and is a fine person and an attorney, so we got the death certificates necessary and had the body cremated and ready for transport back to Lancaster. The old bear had finally left us, but Dad had left specific instructions he also wanted a memorial service to be organized in Lancaster and a Military Funeral with all the bells and whistles and interment in Riverside at the same Military Cemetery where my Mother Kathryn had been laid to rest. So, from Canada, we flew back with the ashes to Lancaster, rented another room for a week and organized the memorial and contacted the relatives, etc. Again Matje was kind of out of it with grief so Barbara and I did most of the organizing and doing.

I also had to get a hold of the Military Cemetery in Riverside and come up with military documentation and arrange for a Military Chaplin, 21 gun salute team and a service site on the premises, etc.. Finally after this 3 week ordeal was over. Barbara and I were exhausted and needed another week off to recover before going back to work.

Except, when I finally got back to Santa Barbara, I found myself losing 2 of my 3 jobs for taking too much time off. So, I was only working a couple of days a week and had racked up a bit of debt with Dad's funeral expenses. But, I had substantial savings so I was not too worried. So Thanksgiving in 2004, was kind of a somber affair. And my bipolar depression started acting up, so many visits to the shrink.

Then on December 17th, 2004, right before Christmas in Santa Barbara, I was involved in an auto accident, which changed everything again. Sitting stopped at a stop sign in town, fiddling with the radio in my small Ford Ranger truck- I was suddenly rear ended by a drunk driver who was going about 50 MPH, according to the police. Pushed me through the intersection into the car in front of me and I ended up in the back seat of my truck with several broken vertebrae in my already compromised back and my neck. They took me to the Hospital and my Doctor told me I was going to need a back fusion surgery with titanium hardware and Neck fusion surgery. Swell-the guy that hit me had no insurance and my insurance company was lagging while I was dying in pain. So, not a very good Christmas- out of work, in pain, waiting for the insurance company to ok major surgery and very depressed.

Barbara cared for me during this time and finally in March 2005, I had the major back surgery and soon after, the neck fusion surgery. Now out of work for a substantial time and possibly for good....

With time slowly passing by recuperating and getting bored with life in general now.....I came up with the bright idea for a new creative project...remodel my house! I did this and it turned out to be a big mistake! Turned a small 3 bedroom, 3 bath house into a large 5 bedroom, 4 bath house. My thinking at the time was to then "flip" the house (sell it quickly after the work" and make a nice profit) on the Real Estate Market in SB. Then move into a small place with Barbara and retire from Dentistry Didn't work out well.....ended up losing money on the deal for a lot of complex reasons which I will explain upon request. But stayed in the very nice house until 2011, when Barbara and I then moved back up to Solvang, where we now reside with 2 cats and a dog.

I'll mention in passing that I did open another Dental Office in 2009-2010, and worked part-time, just to "test" out my back and see some old clients, but after about a year, it was obvious that my back couldn't take anymore abuse (some guys never learn!) so I found young dentist who bought the business.

Ok, now I didn't forget about Daughter Jennifer or Kylee, Devyn and Hudson-it's just that she can tell her own story better than I can, so I'll be brief. Jennifer met and dated Frank Dutra for a few years and they were married on 9/5/2005 and blessed us all with 3 wonderful grandchildren-you know who you are!

I also will not attempt to tell the Carol McCauley (formerly Carol Hull) story as it would be unfair and grossly incomplete in content. Suffice it to say there's 2 sides to every story.

What I will leave you with is this. In addition to the Dutra "clan"; 1) There are tons of Hull cousins, uncles, and aunts, etc. throughout the West Coast in California, Washington State, Idaho and I believe (Steve Hull Junior) Utah (?);2) There are tons of relatives named "Ballas" (my Mother's) residing on the East coast of the U.S. and abroad and the Ballas family farm near Robertsdale, Pennsylvania still exists today and is much as it was when my Mother was born and raised there in the early 1900's. So....seek and ye will find, grandchildren!

Is all of this story really true? Well..you bet...for the most part (I may have flubbed a few dates) and embellished a few stories to make it interesting. But yeah, it's the real deal.

I hope you have enjoyed this short story as much as I have in writing it. Like I said in the beginning- take what you wish and leave the rest.

As for me.....would I do anything different if I could given the chance for a "do over". Maybe not being in my second marriage to Marilyn-maybe. But, naw God had and has a plan for all of us and we play the cards we're dealt-for better or worse sometimes. My life has been full and exciting and I've been blessed many times over. Maybe I'll live into my 80's or 90's like my Grandfather and Father, but perhaps not-who knows? But I do know this.....I have and had a wonderful family of which I'm proud and leave you with love in my heart for all

God bless us all
fondly,

Frank Edgar Hull II
August 2014
Solvang, California

FORREST EDGAR HULL
[------- born: 09/08/1911
5 adopted offspring          STEPHAN NELSON HULL     [          MARRIAGE #1-1937
all married          [ ---born: 03/20/1939------------     --[          divorced- 1946
Steve Hull Jr.          [     died: 11/23/1989          [
Stacy Hull          -------[          [
Robin Hull          [          [
Ryan Hull          [          [
Amber Hull          [     Sandra Bailey          [
          [--- born: 04/10/1945          [-------- Shirley Klogsten


          [ ---Frank Dutra          FORREST EDGAR HULL
KYLEE DUTRA          [          [---MARRIAGE #2
DEVYN DUTRA          ------------- [          [     1947
HUDSON DUTRA          [          FRANK EDGAR HULL II          [  widowed: 1992
          [  JENNIFER ELLEN HULL          [--- born:04/04/1948
          [-- born 02/04/1978          [     Washington, D.C.-------- [
          Inglewood, California     ------------- [          [     married: 08/16/1975          [
          married 09/10/2005          [     divorced:  1987          [  KATHRYN REGINA BALLAS
          divorced: 01/01/2010          [          [---     born: 11/01/1907
          [          place :Robertsdale, Pennsylvania
          [          died: 10/13/1992
          [     Carol Ellen Witt          place: Lancaster, Calif.
          [--- born; 06/19/1947
          Inglewood, Calif.

*prepared by          FORREST EDGAR HULL
Frank E Hull II-08/2014          [--     MARRIAGE #3 -02/04/2002
          [ died:10/21/2004  -Alberta,Canada
          [
          [--   Martje Van Wachem-died 2014

REMARRIAGES OF FRANK E. HULL & CAROL ELLEN WITT


                                    STEVE McCOLLEY
                                    [-- BORN 04/04 1949
LIVE AT 9850 SAN MARCOS -------     [    MARRIED 02/08/1991(SECOND MARRIAGE FOR BOTH)
ROAD, ATASCADERO, CALIF.            [
                                    [--CAROL ELLEN WITT


                                    [--FRANK EDGAR HULL II
                                    [    MARRIED 02/18/2004
                                    [    (THIRD MARRIAGE-DON'T WANT TO TALK ABOUT #2)
                                    [
LIVE AT 95 SIERRA VISTA   -------   [
SOLVANG, CALIFORNIA                 [
                                    [--BARBARA NAPOLEONE GARDNER (GRANDMA ST. BARB.)
                                            BORN 01/16/1948

FAMILY LINE FOR KATHRYN REGINA BALLAS
(FRANK HULL JR.'S MOTHER)

[JOSEF BALLAS (OR SOME EUROPEAN NAME SHORTENED)
[ IMIGRATED FROM AUSTRIA-1900 OR SO-
[AUSTRIAN/CZECOSLAVACIAN ANCESTRY
[ DIED 1943
[
KATRYN REGINA BALLAS--------------   [
(AND 9 BROTHERS AND                  [
SISTERS)                             [
                                     [
                                     [
[ ELIZABETH ?
  (ALSO IMMIGRANT FROM AUSTRIA, BUT OF POLISH ANCESTRY)
   DIED PRIOR TO 1948

Ordinance Codes:
B=Baptized
E=Endowed
P=Sealed to parents
S=Sealed to spouse
C=Children's ordinances

8 HENRY Silas HULL-519--------------------
  BORN:  29 Oct 1831              BEP    2
  PLACE: WESTFORD,OTSEGO,NY
  MARR:  31 Dec 1853    --185
  PLACE:
  DIED:  Aft    1900
  PLACE: (prob.),ISLAND,WA

4 Charles Eugene HULL-14------------------
  BORN:  26 Apr 1859              BE
  PLACE: Joliet,Will,IL
  MARR:   2 Mar 1878(div)   --5
  PLACE: WHEATLAND,Dickinson,KS
  DIED:   4 Jun 1943
  PLACE: San Francisco,S,CA

9 Sarah RAWSON BABCOCK-520------------------
  BORN:
  PLACE:
  DIED:
  PLACE:

2 Frank Edgar HULL-12----------------------
  BORN:  11 Oct 1882          BEP
  PLACE: Abilene,Dickinson,KS
  MARR:  27 Jan 1910    --4
  PLACE: SANTA MONICA,Los Angeles,CA
  DIED:  22 May 1968
  PLACE: Lancaster,Los Angeles,CA

10 Andrew J. HOLSHOUSER-730------------------
   BORN:  Abt    1815/1825
   PLACE: ,,NC
   MARR:  16 Oct 1851   --289
   PLACE: ,Will,IL
   DIED:         1858/1860
   PLACE: Limestone,Kankakee,IL

5 Ida Mae E. HOLSHOUSER-15-----------------
  BORN:  22 Feb 1859
  PLACE: Limestone,Kankakee,IL
  DIED:   8 Dec 1943
  PLACE: ,,CA

11 Sophia VANDECAR-731----------------------
   BORN:  Abt    1832/1834            3
   PLACE: ,ONTARIO,CANADA
   DIED:         1860/1865
   PLACE: Limestone,Kankakee,IL

ver
<=1 Forrest Edgar HULL-8---------------------
  BORN:   8 Sep 1911
  PLACE: Los Angeles,Los Angeles,CA
  MARR:
  PLACE:
  DIED:
  PLACE:
  ------------------------------------------
  Spouse

12 James MCLAUGHLIN-766----------------------
   BORN:
   PLACE:
   MARR:        --300
   PLACE:
   DIED:
   PLACE:

6 Joseph Holt MCLAUGHLIN-20----------------
  BORN:  31 Oct 1861              BE
  PLACE: Bainbridge,Ross,OH
  MARR:  26 Jun 1881    --7
  PLACE:
  DIED:          Sep 1885
  PLACE: English,Crawford,IN

13 MARTHA Jane ROBY-767---------------------
   BORN:
   PLACE:
   DIED:
   PLACE:

3 Margaret May MCLAUGHLIN-13---------------
  BORN:  11 May 1883          BEP
  PLACE: English,Crawford,IN
  DIED:  29 Dec 1957
  PLACE: Los Angeles,Los Angeles,CA

14 John KENNEDY-768---------------------------
   BORN:
   PLACE:
   MARR:        --301
   PLACE:
   DIED:
   PLACE:

7 Margaret Ann KENNEDY-21------------------
  BORN:  16 Jun 1862
  PLACE: ,,GA
  DIED:   2 Jul 1936
  PLACE: Edinburg,Johnson,IN

15 MARTHA JANE/ANN CAVERNY-769-------------
   BORN:
   PLACE:
   DIED:
   PLACE:

Name and address of submitter:
STEPHEN HULL (#5155)
C/O LINEAGES, INC.
P.O. BOX 417
SALT LAKE CITY, UT  84110
Phone:(801) 531-9297